Editor
Sara Connolly

Editor in Chief
Ina Massler Levin, M.A.

Creative Director
Karen J. Goldfluss, M.S. Ed.

Cover Artist
Brenda DiAntonis

Imaging
Leonard P. Swierski

Publisher

Mary D. Smith, M.S. Ed.

Grades 4-5

Using GOOGLE DOCS™ in the Classroom

Step-by-step directions allow students to Create and Collaborate on:

- word processing documents
- spreadsheets
- forms
- drawings
- presentations

Teacher Created Resources

Author

Steve Butz

Teacher Created Resources
6421 Industry Way
Westminster, CA 92683
www.teachercreated.com

ISBN: 978-1-4206-2930-9

© 2012 Teacher Created Resou
Made in U.S.A.

D1275859

Teacher Created Resources

Table of Contents

Word Processing Activities

Spreadsheet Activities

Drawing Activities

Form Activities

Presentation Activities

Introduction

Using Google Docs in the Classroom was written for teachers who would like to utilize the Google Docs™ program to enhance their elementary school curriculum. Google Docs is a free online software suite that gives students access to word-processing, spreadsheet, presentation, and drawing programs. With Google Docs, students can create, edit, share, and collaborate on documents with their peers. All files are stored by Google and are accessible from any computer that has Internet access, giving students the opportunity to continue to work on their school projects from home. The only requirement for use is an email address. (If your students do not have email addresses, contact your school's technology coordinator to discuss ways to provide free email solutions for your students.)

The activities in this book were designed for use in a computer lab or classroom setting where students have access to online computers. Each activity has been successfully used in the classroom and was designed to be completed in a 45-minute computer lab session. Each activity includes the overall purpose of the lesson, learning objectives, materials required, and detailed step-by-step procedures, along with informative pictures that show you exactly what to do. No knowledge of software applications is required to teach the activities contained in this book.

The book is arranged in five sections that correlate to the five different types of software applications available in Google Docs: Word Processing, Spreadsheets, Drawings, Forms, and Presentations. The 16 activities contained in this book address many different ways in which elementary educators can utilize software. This offers teachers the opportunity to confidently take classes into the computer lab and use Google Docs to present a well-rounded lesson.

Although each lesson contains specific subject matter, all labs in this book can be easily adapted to fit your specific lesson plans by using your own data. The labs are designed to illustrate the many ways that computers can be used in your classroom to reinforce your specific topic of study and may provide you with a variety of ways to incorporate technology into your curriculum.

Get started with Google Docs by going to **http://docs.google.com**.
Sign in with your Google account, or click on **create an account now** to sign up using your email address.

Google Docs™ and Collaboration

One of the advantages of using the Google Docs program is that it provides students with a method of collaborating on projects. What this means is that students can grant specified people access to their online documents. This access can allow others to either read or edit documents. If you grant edit permission to a document, then students can work on the same document simultaneously. This is especially useful for group projects using presentation software. Students can grant others access to their documents by clicking the link to the **Sharing settings**. (See Figure A.)

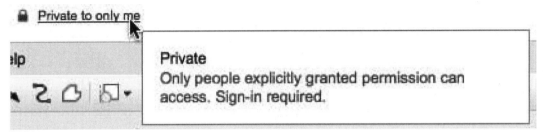

Figure A

Under the Sharing Settings window, you can add the email addresses of people you wish to either view or edit your documents. Select **Can view** or **Can edit** depending on what you would like them to be able to do. You can also send them an email that provides a link to access your document. (See Figure B.)

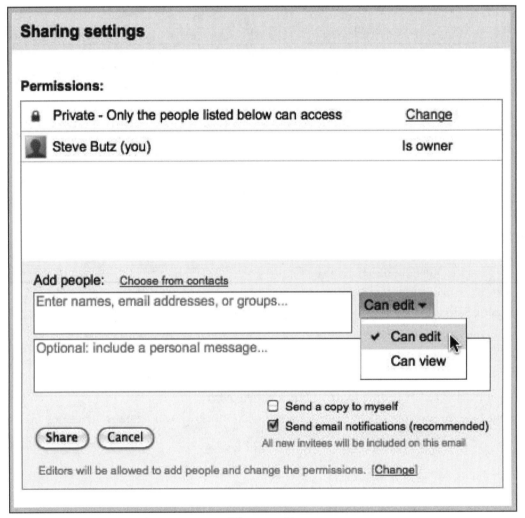

Figure B

Formatting Drill

Activity 1

Objectives

Each student will utilize the Google Docs word-processing application to edit and format a document.

Benchmarks for Technology Standards

Students will know the characteristics, uses, and basic features of word-processing programs, including:
- opening a file
- applying formatting to text
- editing, copying, moving, and saving text
- formatting text by centering lines, using tabs, and forming paragraphs
- changing the line spacing of text

Learning Objectives

At the end of this lesson, students will be able to:
1. insert, align, underline, and bold text in a document
2. change the font of text in a document
3. change font size, style, and color
4. change the indent spacing
5. alter the line spacing of a paragraph
6. create a bulleted list

Variations

This activity was written using the information about the unusual animal known as the pangolin. You may choose to use another short paragraph about a different subject that may better fit your curriculum. An example of a completed document is shown in Figure 1-1.

What is a Pangolin?

A pangolin is a mammal that looks like a giant anteater. It is about three feet long and is covered in grayish-brown scales. A pangolin has a long, sticky tongue that it uses to catch insects to eat.

The pangolin is a nocturnal animal that comes out to feed between midnight and dawn. It has large digging claws on its front feet. A pangolin uses its claws to dig into termite mounds and create big burrows in which it lives.

PANGOLINS LIVE IN TROPICAL RAIN FORESTS NEAR THE EQUATOR IN AFRICA. THEY CAN EAT OVER 200,000 ANTS AND TERMITES IN ONE NIGHT. WHEN THE PANGOLIN IS THREATENED, IT WILL CURL UP IN A BALL AND PROTECT ITSELF.

- *Pangolins have no external ears.*
- *They live near water.*
- *Pangolins can stand up on their tails.*

Figure 1-1

Formatting Drill *(cont.)*

Activity 1

Procedure

1. Sign in to Google Docs.
2. Go to **Create** and choose **Document**.
3. Click into the **Untitled document** box at the upper-left corner of the page (see Figure 1-2) and type your last name, then the title "Pangolin Report." Click **OK** in the **Rename Document** window.

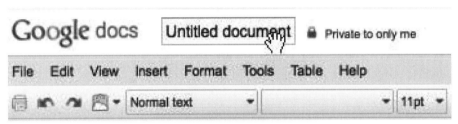

Figure 1-2

4. Next, type the following paragraphs into your document:

What is a Pangolin?

A pangolin is a mammal that looks like a giant anteater. It is about three feet long and is covered in grayish-brown scales. A pangolin has a long, sticky tongue that it uses to catch insects to eat.

The pangolin is a nocturnal animal that comes out to feed between midnight and dawn. It has large digging claws on its front feet. A pangolin uses its claws to dig into termite mounds and create big burrows in which it lives.

Pangolins live in tropical rain forests near the equator in Africa. They can eat over 200,000 ants and termites in one night. When the pangolin is threatened, it will curl up into a ball and protect itself.

5. Now highlight the title, and center it by using the **Center align** button (see Figure 1-3).

What is a Pangolin?

Figure 1-3

Formatting Drill *(cont.)*

Activity 1

6. Next, keep the title highlighted, and increase its font size to **14pt** using the **Font size** button. Also make the title bold and underlined by using the **Bold** button (**B**) and the **Underline** button (**U**) (Figure 1-4).

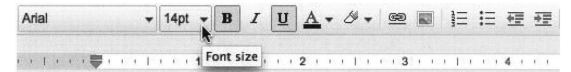

What is a Pangolin?

Figure 1-4

7. Now you are going to change the indent for the first line of the first paragraph. Click in front of the "A" at the beginning of the first paragraph. Hit the **tab** key on your keyboard. The first line of your paragraph should now be indented. You can change how far an indent is by using the **First Line Indent** tool. Click on the tool, and slide it to the one-inch mark on the ruler. This will change the indent to one inch. (See Figure 1-5.)

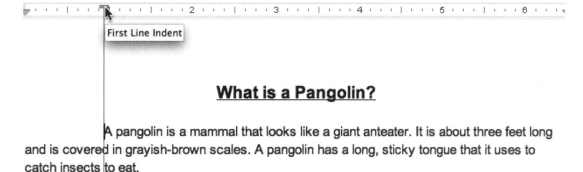

What is a Pangolin?

A pangolin is a mammal that looks like a giant anteater. It is about three feet long and is covered in grayish-brown scales. A pangolin has a long, sticky tongue that it uses to catch insects to eat.

Figure 1-5

8. Now you are going to align the first paragraph to the right margin and also italicize it. Highlight the entire first paragraph and click the **Right align** button. Then click the **Italic** (*I*) button (Figure 1-6).

What is a Pangolin?

A pangolin is a mammal that looks like a giant anteater. It is about three feet long and is covered in grayish-brown scales. A pangolin has a long, sticky tongue that it uses to catch insects to eat.

Figure 1-6

9. Next, change the font of the first paragraph to **Droid Sans**.

10. Now you are going to use the Justify command. Justify makes your paragraph align to both the left and right margins of your page, making your text like a box. This is a common alignment used in books, magazines, and newspapers. Highlight the second paragraph and click the **Justify** button (Figure 1-7).

Figure 1-7

11. Next, keep the second paragraph highlighted and change the font to **Cambria** and increase its size to **12pt**.

12. Now highlight the third paragraph and change its font to **Syncopate**, size **12pt**. Next, you will change the spacing between sentences. With the paragraph still highlighted, click the **Line spacing** button and choose **2.0**. (See Figure 1-8.)

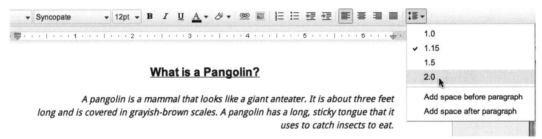

Figure 1-8

13. Next, you will add a bulleted list to your document. To do this, click after the period at the end of the last sentence in the third paragraph. Hit the **Enter** key on your keyboard once, then click on the **Bulleted list** button (Figure 1-9).

Figure 1-9

14. A bullet point should appear. Now type the following Pangolin fact after the bullet: "Pangolins have no external ears." Hit the **Enter** key on your keyboard to create another bullet. Type the following fact: "They live near water." Finally, add a third bullet and type: "Pangolins can stand up on their tails."

15. To turn off the bulleted list, hit **Enter** and then hit the **Bulleted list** button again.

16. Highlight your list, and change the font to **Corsiva**.

17. Your project is now complete!

Pictures and Tables

Activity 2

Objectives

Each student will use the Google Docs word-processing application to create and format a table and insert images.

Benchmarks for Technology Standards

Students will know the characteristics, uses, and basic features of word-processing programs, including:

- opening a file
- applying formatting to text
- editing, copying, moving, saving, and printing text

Learning Objectives

At the end of this lesson, students will be able to:

1. insert a table into a document
2. format a table
3. insert and format text within a table
4. insert an image into a document
5. change an image's alignment and size
6. change the background color within a table

Variations

An example of a completed project is shown in Figure 2-1. This activity uses leaf identification, but you may choose to substitute it with another type of identification that better suits your curriculum. If you do choose to alter the activity, make sure to check the image search function to assure the images are there for you to use and are appropriate.

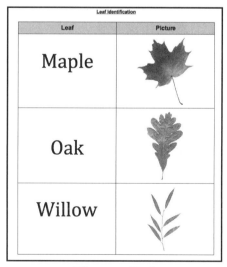

Figure 2-1

Pictures and Tables (cont.)

Activity 2

Procedure

1. Sign in to Google Docs.
2. Go to **Create** and choose **Document**.
3. Click into the **Untitled document** box at the upper-left corner of the page (see Figure 2-2) and type your last name, then the title "Leaf ID." Click **OK** in the **Rename Document** window.

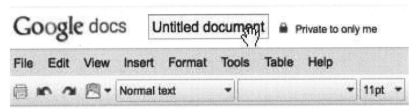

Figure 2-2

4. Next, type the following title at the top of your document: "Leaf Identification."
5. Highlight the title and center it using the **Center align** button (Figure 2-3).

Figure 2-3

6. Make your title bold and underlined by using the **Bold (B)** and **Underline (U)** buttons. Click at the end of the title to remove the highlighting. Click the **Bold (B)** and **Underline (U)** buttons again to turn them off.
7. Hit the **Enter** key on your keyboard and choose the **Table** menu. From the Table menu, select a table that has two columns and three rows. (See Figure 2-4.)

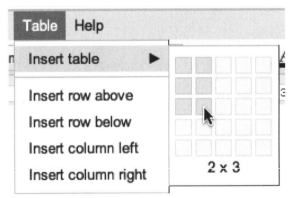

Figure 2-4

8. Tables are made of cells. A cell is a location within a table where a row meets a column. Click into the top left cell of your table and type the following label: "Leaf." Next, hit the **Tab** key on your keyboard. This will automatically move you over to the next cell within your table. Now type "Picture."

9. Now highlight both titles in the table, increase their font size to **14pt**, and make them both bold by using the **Bold** button (**B**). Also use the **Center align** button to center them within their cells. (See Figure 2-5.)

Leaf Identification

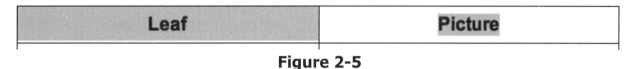

Leaf	Picture

Figure 2-5

10. Next, click into the cell below the word "Leaf." Type "Maple." Hit the **Tab** key on your keyboard to move over to the cell below the word "Picture."

11. Now you are going to insert a picture into the cell. Click the **Insert** menu and choose **Image**. You can navigate to an image from your computer and insert it, or you can use Google's Image Search function.

12. If you want to use Google Image Search, click **Google Image Search** and type "maple leaf" into the search box. Click the **Search images** button and click on an image of a maple leaf. Now click the **Select** button.

13. Next, you will have to resize the image so it fits within the cell. Click on the image to show its anchor points. Anchor points are the small dots that allow you to change the size of the image. Click on the anchor point at the upper-left corner of the image, and drag it down toward the bottom-right corner of your table until the image fits within the cell (Figure 2-6).

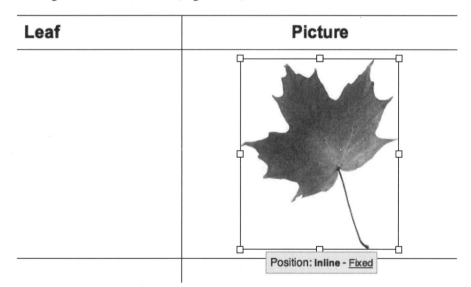

Figure 2-6

14. Next, click back in front of the word "Maple" and hit the **Enter** key on your keyboard several times to center the text within the cell. Now highlight "Maple" and increase its font size to **48**. Also change the font to **Cambria**.

15. Now click into the cell below the word "Maple" and type "Oak." Hit the **Tab** key on your keyboard to move over one cell to the right, and then insert another picture, using the **Insert** menu as in steps 11 and 12. This time type "oak leaf" in the **Google Image Search** box.

~~~~~~

16. Click on an image of an oak leaf and hit the **Select** button. Click on the image and use an anchor point to resize it so the image is the same size as the maple leaf image.

17. Next, click back in front of the word "Oak" and hit the **Enter** key on your keyboard several times to center the text within the cell. Now highlight "Oak" and increase its font size to **48**. Also change the font to **Cambria**.

18. Now you will add another row to your table so you can enter another picture and label of a leaf. To do this, right-click on your mouse or trackpad (or control-click if you are using a Mac) in the cell labeled "Oak." This will bring up a menu, and you should choose **Insert row below**. (See Figure 2-7.)

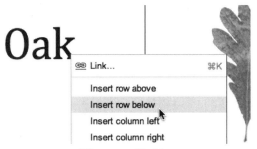

Figure 2-7

19. Repeat steps 15, 16, and 17 for willow leaves, using "willow leaf" as your image search term.

20. Once you have completed all of the steps for inserting an image and label for a willow leaf, click and highlight the cells with the words "Leaf" and "Picture." With the cells still highlighted, right-click on your mouse or trackpad (or control-click if you are using a Mac) and select **Table properties** (Figure 2-8).

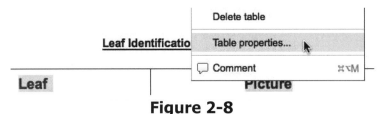

Figure 2-8

21. Next, in the **Table Properties** box, choose **Cell**, and select the **Background color** box. Choose the light gray box and click **OK** (Figure 2-9).

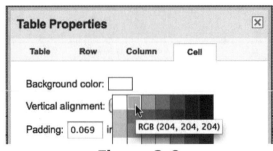

Figure 2-9

22. If you have more time, you may add more leaves and labels to your table. Your project is complete!

All About Me

Activity 3

Objectives

Each student will use the Google Docs word-processing application to create a document about himself or herself.

Benchmarks for Technology Standards

Students will know the characteristics, uses, and basic features of computer software programs, including:

- knowing the common features and uses of desktop publishing and word-processing software
- knowing that documents can be created, designed, and formatted
- using a word processor to print text

Learning Objectives

At the end of this lesson, students will be able to:

1. create a new word-processing document
2. enter text into a document
3. format font size and style
4. change the font of text in a document
5. alter the color of a font
6. insert and format an image into a document
7. use keyboard commands to format text
8. add a header to a document
9. print a document

Before the Computer

Before you begin this assignment you should take a digital picture of each student that they can then insert into their documents. Place the images in a class folder so that students can access them when they are working on this assignment. An example of a completed document is shown in Figure 3-1.

All About Me *(cont.)*

Activity 3

All About Me

by Charlotte Student

Physical Characteristics: My hair is blond and my eyes are blue.

Favorite Color: Red

My Family: My dad (Doug), my mom (Ellen), and my brother (Joe).

What I Want to Be When I Grow Up: A dancer

My Pets: I have two dogs: Tucker and Henry

Favorite Hobby or Sport: Soccer

Favorite Book: Ripley's Believe it or Not!

Favorite TV Show: SpongeBob

Figure 3-1

All About Me *(cont.)*

Activity 3

Procedure

1. Sign in to Google Docs.

2. Go to **Create** and choose **Document**.

3. Click into the **Untitled document** box at the upper left corner of the page and type your last name, then the title "All About Me." (See Figure 3-2.) Click **OK** in the **Rename Document** window.

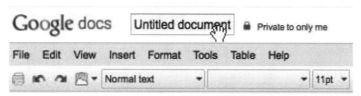

Figure 3-2

4. Type the following title at the top of your document: "All About Me." Highlight the title by clicking and dragging over it. Then center it by clicking on the **Center align** icon. Your title should now be centered.

5. Increase the font size of your title by choosing the **Font Size** button and selecting **24 pt**. Also change the font to **Garamond** (Figure 3-3).

Figure 3-3

6. Next, click at the end of the title and hit **Enter** on your keyboard, type "by," and enter your first name and last name. Highlight what you just typed and reduce its font size to **14 pt** (Figure 3-4).

All About Me

by Charlotte Student

Figure 3-4

7. Hit the **Enter** key twice to move down two lines. Click the **Left align** button to move your cursor to the left margin (Figure 3-5).

Figure 3-5

All About Me (cont.)

Activity 3

8. Now type the following: "Physical Characteristics." Hit the colon key on your keyboard (:), then hit the **Tab** key once. Next, type a description of your hair and eye color (Figure 3-6).

9. Next, highlight just word or words that describe the color of your hair, and click the **Text color** button. Change the color of your text to the same color as your hair (Figure 3-6).

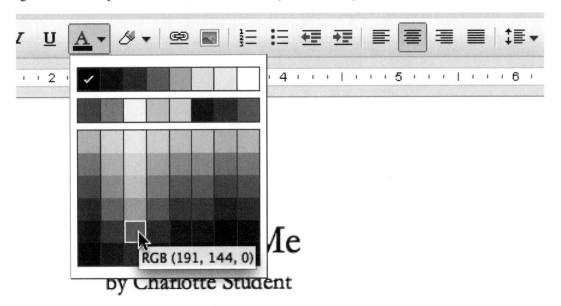

Figure 3-6

10. Now highlight the word or words that describe your eye color and change its font color to match the color of your eyes.

11. Next, click after the words that describe your physical characteristics and hit **Enter**. Then click the **Center align** button.

12. Now you are going to insert a picture of yourself into your document. To do this, choose the **Insert** menu and select **Image**. Next, click on the **Upload** button and then click **Choose File**. You will now navigate to your class folder to find your picture (Figure 3-7).

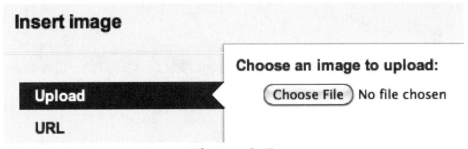

Figure 3-7

13. Once you locate your picture file, click the **Open** button. Your image should now be inserted into your document.

14. Next, you will have to resize the image so it is the correct size. Click on the image to show its anchor points. Anchor points are the small dots that allow you to change the size of the image. You can click on one of the corner anchor points and drag it to make the image smaller or larger (Figure 3-8).

Figure 3-8

15. Now click after the picture and hit the **Enter** key on your keyboard twice to move two lines below your picture. Click the **Left align** button to move your cursor over to the left margin.

16. Type "Favorite Color:" next. Hit the **Tab** key and then type the name of your favorite color.

17. When you are done, highlight the color word and change its color to your favorite color (Figure 3-9).

Favorite Color: Red

Figure 3-9

18. Now highlight the words "Physical Characteristics:" and make them bold and underlined using the **Bold** (**B**) and **Underline** (**U**) buttons (Figure 3-10). Do the same for "Favorite Color:"

Figure 3-10

19. To complete your project, add and fill out the following information about yourself.

My Family:	**What I Want to Be When I Grow Up:**
My Pets:	**Favorite Hobby or Sport:**
Favorite Book:	**Favorite TV Show:**

20. Your project is now complete!

Changing Daylight

Activity 4

Objectives

Each student will utilize the Google Docs spreadsheet application to create a line chart showing the changing hours of daylight throughout the year.

Benchmarks for Technology Standards

Students will know the characteristics, uses, and basic features of computer software programs, including:

- knowing the common features and uses of spreadsheets
- using spreadsheet software to update, add, and delete data, and to produce charts

Learning Objectives

At the end of this lesson, students will be able to:

1. know the various terms associated with spreadsheets including rows, columns, and cells

2. enter data into a spreadsheet

3. adjust the width of a selected column

4. change the alignment of data within a cell

5. change the style of data within a cell

6. create and format a line chart from data entered within a spreadsheet

Variations

This activity is written using the average monthly daylight hours for the middle northern latitudes. If you want to alter this activity to make a graph showing the length of daylight for your location, you can use the following website: **http://www.timeanddate.com**. Just scroll down to the Sun and Moon Calculators section, and click on the Sunrise and Sunset Calculator link. You can then choose the name of the closest city to find the day lengths for each month. An example of a completed project is shown in Figure 4-1.

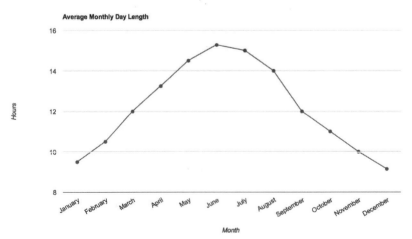

Figure 4-1

Changing Daylight *(cont.)*

Activity 4

Procedure

1. Open a new spreadsheet document using Google Docs by going to **Create** and choosing **Spreadsheet**.

2. At the top of the document in the **Unsaved Spreadsheet** box, type your last name and then the title "Day Length Line Chart" (see Figure 4-2). Click **OK** in the **Rename Document** window.

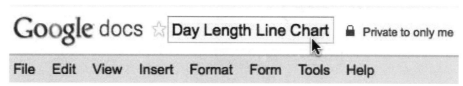

Figure 4-2

3. Spreadsheets are made up of columns that are identified by letters (A, B, C, etc.) and rows that are identified by numbers (1, 2, 3, etc.).

4. The location within a spreadsheet where a column meets a row is called a *cell* and is identified by both a letter and number (Figure 4-3).

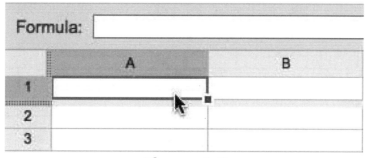

Figure 4-3

5. Click into cell **A1** and enter the following column label: "Month."

6. Next, increase its font size to **12 pt** by clicking the **Font size** button and also use the **Bold** button (**B**) to make the font bold.

7. Now center your label within its cell by using the **Align** button (Figure 4-4).

Figure 4-4

8. Hit the **Tab** key on your keyboard to move you over to cell **B1**. Now type the following column heading: "Day Length (hours)." Center the label in its cell, increase its font size to **12**, and make it bold.

Changing Daylight *(cont.)*

Activity 4

9. Next, you will have to widen column B so that its label fits. To do this, take your cursor and bring it between columns B and C, then click and drag to the right (Figure 4-5) until the text fits on one line.

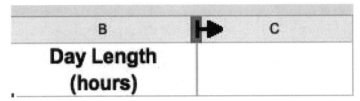

Figure 4-5

10. Now use the information in the following data table to input the day length and month into your spreadsheet:

Month	Day Length (hours)
January	9.5
February	10.5
March	12
April	13.25
May	14.5
June	15.28
July	15
August	14
September	12
October	11
November	10
December	9.15

11. Once your data is entered, highlight it by clicking and dragging over it, then center it using the **Align** button (Figure 4-6).

Figure 4-6

Changing Daylight (cont.)

Activity 4

Spreadsheets

12. With your data still highlighted, change the font size to **12** using the **Font size** button (Figure 4-7).

Figure 4-7

13. Next, you are going to use your data to make a line chart. Click into cell **A1**, then go to the **Insert** menu and choose "Chart." You can also hit the **Insert chart** button (Figure 4-8).

Figure 4-8

14. You will now use the **Chart Editor** window to create a line chart. Make sure there is a check mark in the **Use row 1 as headers** box, then click the **Charts** link (Figure 4-9).

Figure 4-9

15. Next, under **Charts**, click on **Line** and select **line chart**, which is the one above **smooth line chart** (Figure 4-10).

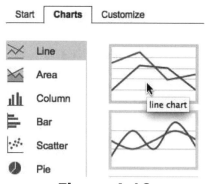

Figure 4-10

Changing Daylight *(cont.)*

Activity 4

Spreadsheets

16. A preview of your chart will now appear in the **Preview** window. Now click on the **Customize** link (Figure 4-11).

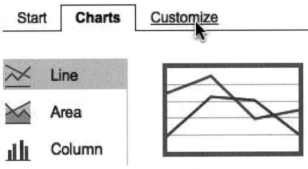

Figure 4-11

17. In the **Customize** window, click in the **Chart title** box and type, "Average Monthly Day Length," then click out of that box. The chart title should now appear above your chart. Next, click on the **Name** link (Figure 4-12).

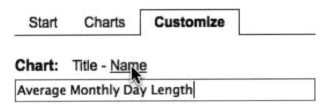

Figure 4-12

18. This will give your chart a name that is linked to your spreadsheet data. Type the following in the **Chart Name** box: "Line Chart."

19. Next, under **Layout: Legend**, click the **None** button to remove the legend from your chart (Figure 4-13). You will not need a legend when the chart is only plotting one set of data.

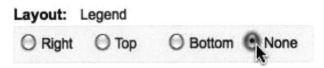

Figure 4-13

20. Now click into the **Axis –Vertical** box and type the name of your vertical axis, which is "Hours." Next, click the **Horizontal** axis link. (Figure 4-14).

Figure 4-14

Changing Daylight *(cont.)*

Activity 4

21. In the **Horizontal Axis** box, type the following label: "Month."

22. Next, under **Style**, click the **Point** link (Figure 4-15).

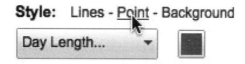

Figure 4-15

23. Click the **Point** menu and choose **Medium** (Figure 4-16).

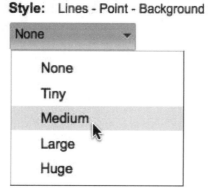

Figure 4-16

24. Now that your chart is set up, click the **Insert** button located at the bottom-right corner of the **Chart Editor** window.

25. Finally, to display your chart as its own page within your spreadsheet, click on the chart, and then select the **Line Chart** menu located in the upper-left corner of the chart (Figure 4-17).

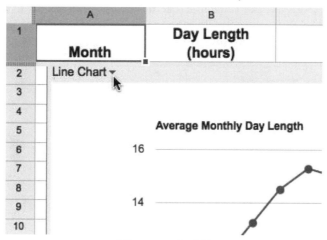

Figure 4-17

26. Under the **Line Chart** menu, select the **Move to own sheet**… option. This will insert your chart on its own page. Your project is now complete!

Ocean Temperatures

Activity 5

Objectives

Each student will utilize the Google Docs spreadsheet application to create a column chart showing the changes in the average mean temperature of the ocean from 1880 to the present.

Benchmarks for Technology Standards

Students will know the characteristics, uses, and basic features of computer software programs, including:

- knowing the common features and uses of spreadsheets
- using spreadsheet software to update, add, and delete data, and to produce charts

Learning Objectives

At the end of this lesson, students will be able to:

1. know the various terms associated with spreadsheets, including rows, columns, and cells
2. enter data into a spreadsheet
3. adjust the width of a selected column
4. change the alignment of data within a cell
5. change the style of data within a cell
6. use the Autofill function to enter data into a column with a spreadsheet
7. create and format a column chart from data entered within a spreadsheet

Before the Computer

This activity was written using the average mean change in ocean temperature from the period of 1880 to 2010. It is important to explain to your students that the chart does not show the actual temperature of the ocean, but the change in temperature from the global average calculated between the years 1880–2010. This allows scientists to identify trends in the change in global ocean temperatures over time. An example of a completed project is shown in Figure 5-1.

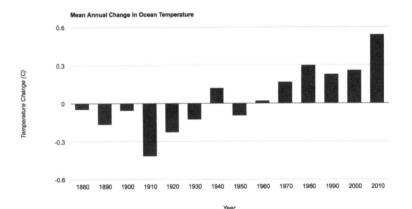

Figure 5-1

Ocean Temperatures (cont.)

Activity 5

Procedure

1. Open a new spreadsheet document using Google Docs.

2. At the top of the document in the **Unsaved spreadsheet** box, type your last name and then the title "Ocean Temperature Change Chart." Click **OK** in the **Save Spreadsheet** window.

3. Spreadsheets are made up of columns that are identified by letters (A, B, C, etc.) and rows that are identified by numbers (1, 2, 3, etc.).

4. The location within a spreadsheet where a column meets a row is called a *cell* and is identified by both a letter and number (Figure 5-2).

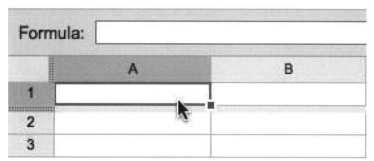

Figure 5-2

5. Click into cell **A1** and type the following label: "Year."

6. Next, hit the **Tab** key on your keyboard. This will move you over into cell B1. Now type "Change in Temperature (C)."

7. Click and drag over cells **A1** and **B1** to highlight them. Use the **Align** button to center the labels in their cells and the **Bold** button (B) to make them bold (Figure 5-3).

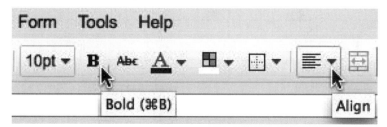

Figure 5-3

8. Now you will have to widen column B so the label will fit. To do this, take your cursor and bring it to the line between column B and C at the top of the spreadsheet. Then click and drag it to the right until the entire label fits on one line (Figure 5-4).

Figure 5-4

9. Next, click into cell **A2** and type "1880." Now hit the **Enter** key on your keyboard. This will take you down to cell A3. Type "1890."

Spreadsheets

10. Next, you are going to use the autofill function to automatically fill in the remaining years in column **A**. Click and drag over cells **A2** and **A3** to highlight them.

11. With the cells still highlighted, move your cursor to the bottom-right corner of cell **A3** until the cursor changes into a cross (Figure 5-5).

	A	B
1	**Year**	**Change in Temperature (C)**
2	1880	
3	1890	
4		
5		

Figure 5-5

12. Now click and drag down until you get to cell **A15**. Let go of the mouse, and the years should have automatically been inserted into your spreadsheet up to 2010.

13. Next, enter the change in temperature for the oceans using the data below.

Year	Change in Temperature (C)
1880	-0.05
1890	-0.17
1900	-0.06
1910	-0.42
1920	-0.23
1930	-0.13
1940	0.12
1950	-0.10
1960	0.02
1970	0.17
1980	0.30
1990	0.23
2000	0.26
2010	0.54

14. Once your data is entered, click and drag over both columns **A** and **B** to highlight them and use the **Align** button to center the data in the cells.

15. Next, click into cell **A1**, go to the "**Insert**" menu, and choose "**Chart**." You can also click on the **Insert chart...** button (Figure 5-6).

Figure 5-6

16. You will now use the **Chart Editor** window to create a column chart. Make sure there is a check mark in the **Use row 1 as headers** box and also in the **Use column A as labels** box, then click the **Charts** link (Figure 5-7).

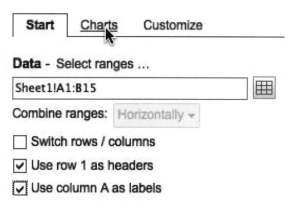

Figure 5-7

17. Next, under **Charts** click on **Column** and select **column chart**, which is the one above **stacked column chart** (Figure 5-8).

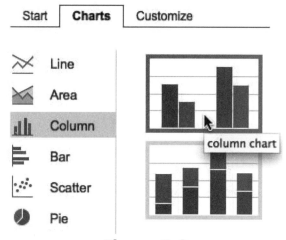

Figure 5-8

18. A preview of your chart will now appear in the **Preview** window. Now click on the **Customize** link.

19. In the **Customize** window, click in the **Chart title** box and type "Mean Annual Change in Ocean Temperatures" (Figure 5-9). Then click out of that box. The chart title should now appear above your chart.

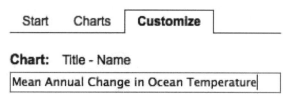

Figure 5-9

20. Next, under **Layout: Legend**, click the **None** button to remove the legend from your chart. You will not need a legend when the chart is only plotting one set of data.

21. Now click into the **Axis: Vertical** box and type the name of your vertical axis, which is "Temperature Change (C)." Next, click the **Horizontal** axis link. (Figure 5-10).

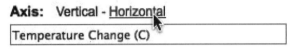

Axis: Vertical - Horizontal

Temperature Change (C)

Figure 5-10

22. In the **Horizontal Axis** box, type the label "Year."

23. Next, under **Style**, click the color box and change the column colors to green (Figure 5-11).

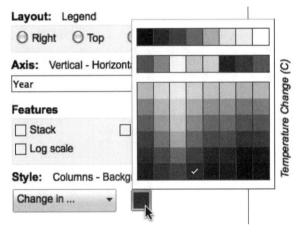

Figure 5-11

24. Now that your chart has been set up, click the **Insert** button located at the bottom-right corner of the **Chart Editor** window.

25. Finally, to display your chart as its own page within your spreadsheet, click on the chart and select the **Chart 1** menu located in the upper-left corner of the chart (Figure 5-12).

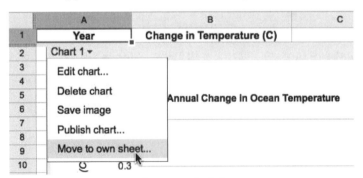

Figure 5-12

26. Under the **Chart 1** menu, select the **Move to own sheet**… option. This will insert your chart on its own page. Your project is now complete!

Earth's Water

Activity 6

Objectives

Each student will utilize the Google Docs spreadsheet application to create a gauge chart showing the distribution of Earth's water.

Benchmarks for Technology Standards

Students will know the characteristics, uses, and basic features of computer software programs, including:

- knowing the common features and uses of spreadsheets
- using spreadsheet software to update, add, and delete data, and to produce charts

Learning Objectives

At the end of this lesson, students will be able to:

1. know the various terms associated with spreadsheets, including rows, columns, and cells

2. enter data into a spreadsheet

3. adjust the width of a selected column

4. change the alignment of data within a cell

5. change the style of data within a cell

6. change the appearance of data to display as a percentage

7. create and format a gauge chart from data entered within a spreadsheet

Variations

This activity was written using the distribution of water on Earth, but any data that is in the form of a percentage out of 100 can be substituted to better fit your curriculum. Just make sure you enter your data in the form of a decimal if you plan to alter this activity. An example of a completed project is shown in Figure 6-1.

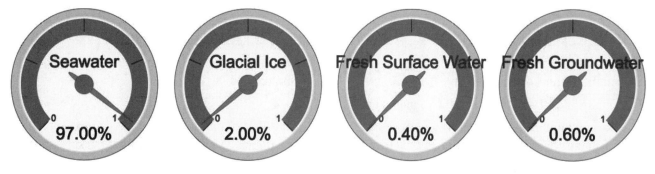

Figure 6-1

Earth's Water (cont.)

Activity 6

Procedure

1. Open a new spreadsheet document using Google Docs.

2. At the top of the document in the **Unsaved spreadsheet** box, type your last name and the title "Earth's Water Gauge Chart." Click **OK** in the **Save Spreadsheet** window.

3. Spreadsheets are made up of columns that are identified by letters (A, B, C, etc.) and rows that are identified by numbers (1, 2, 3, etc.).

4. The location within a spreadsheet where a column meets a row is called a *cell* and is identified by both a letter and number (Figure 6-2).

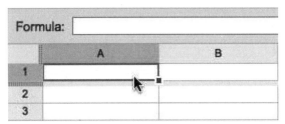

Figure 6-2

5. Click into cell **A1** and type the following label: "Earth's Water."

6. Next, hit the **Tab** key on your keyboard. This will move you over into cell **B1**. Now type "Percentage."

7. Click and drag over cells **A1** and **B1** to highlight them. Use the **Align** button to center the labels in their cells and the **Bold** button (**B**) to make them bold (Figure 6-3).

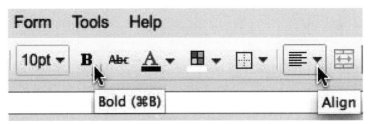

Figure 6-3

8. Next, click into cell **A2** and type "Seawater." Now hit the **Enter** key on your keyboard. This will take you down to cell **A3**. Type "Glacial Ice."

9. Hit the **Enter** key again and type "Fresh Surface Water" into cell **A4**.

10. Finally, in cell **A5**, type "Fresh Groundwater."

11. Now you will have to widen column A so that "Fresh Surface Water" will fit on one line within the cell. To do this, take your cursor and bring it to the line between columns A and B at the top of the spreadsheet. Then click and drag to the right until the entire title fits on one line (Figure 6-4).

Figure 6-4

Earth's Water *(cont.)*

Activity 6

12. Now finish entering the rest of the data using the following information:

Earth's Water	Percentage
Seawater	0.97
Glacial Ice	0.02
Fresh Surface Water	0.004
Fresh Groundwater	0.006

13. Next, you are going to convert the numbers so they display as percentages. To do this, highlight the numbers by clicking and dragging over them.

14. Next, click the **Format as percent** button (Figure 6-5).

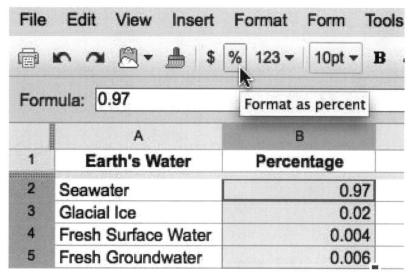

Figure 6-5

15. You can also change the format of numbers in a cell by clicking the **More formats** button (Figure 6-6).

Figure 6-6

16. Next, click into cell **A1**, go to the **Insert** menu, and choose **Chart**, or click on the **Insert chart...** button (Figure 6-7).

Figure 6-7

Earth's Water *(cont.)*

Activity 6

17. You will now use the **Chart Editor** window to create a column chart. Make sure there is a check mark in the **Use row 1 as headers** box.

18. Click on **Charts**, select **More**, and choose **gauge**, which is the option above **organizational chart** (Figure 6-8).

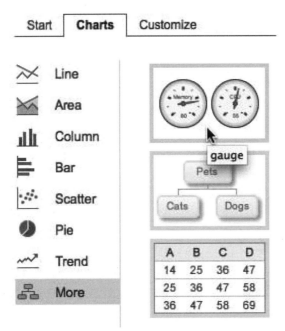

Figure 6-8

19. A preview of your chart will appear in the **Preview** window. Now click on the **Customize** link.

20. In the **Customize** window, click in the **Chart: Name** box and type "Earth's Water."

21. Next, under **Gauge range**, set the minimum value to **0** and the maximum value to **1** (Figure 6-9).

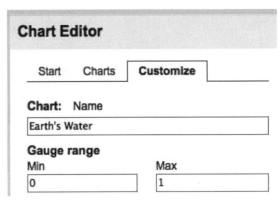

Figure 6-9

Earth's Water (cont.)

Activity 6

22. Next, you can change the color of the gauges. To change them to green, go to **Colored ranges** and click in the **green** section. Set the minimum to "0" and the maximum to "1" (Figure 6-10). Then click out of that box.

Colored ranges

Min	Max
0	1

Min	Max
0	0

Min	Max
0	0

Figure 6-10

23. Now that your chart has been set up, click the **Insert** button located at the bottom-right corner of the **Chart Editor** window.

24. Finally, to display your chart as its own page within your spreadsheet, click on the chart and select the **Earth's Water** menu located in the upper-left corner of the chart (Figure 6-11).

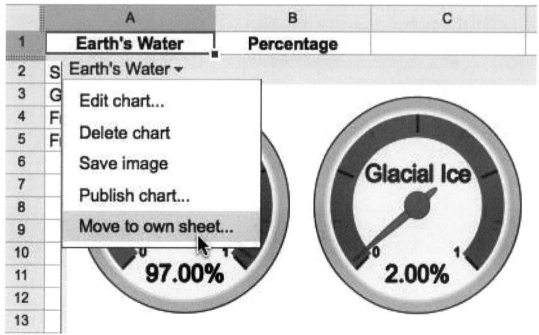

Figure 6-11

25. Under the **Earth's Water** menu, select the **Move to own sheet...** option. This will insert your chart on its own page. Your project is now complete!

Where Does Our Electricity Come From?

Activity 7

Objectives

Each student will utilize the Google Docs spreadsheet application to create a pie chart showing the sources of electricity in the United States.

Benchmarks for Technology Standards

Students will know the characteristics, uses, and basic features of computer software programs, including:

- knowing the common features and uses of spreadsheets
- using spreadsheet software to update, add, and delete data, and to produce charts

Learning Objectives

At the end of this lesson, students will be able to:

1. know the various terms associated with spreadsheets, including rows, columns, and cells
2. enter data into a spreadsheet
3. adjust the width of a selected column
4. change the alignment of data within a cell
5. change the style of data within a cell
6. use the sort function to sort data within a column
7. change the format of numbers to display as percentages
8. create and format a pie chart from data entered within a spreadsheet

Variations

This activity was written using the various sources of electricity in the United States, but any data that is in the form of a percentage out of 100 can be substituted to better fit your curriculum. Just make sure you enter your data in the form of a decimal if you plan to alter this activity. An example of a completed project is shown in Figure 7-1.

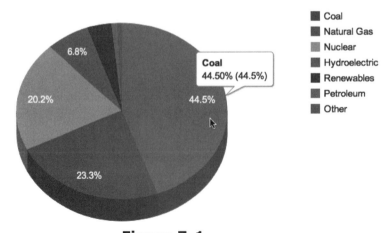

Figure 7-1

Where Does Our Electricity Come From? *(cont.)*

Activity 7

Procedure

1. Open a new spreadsheet document using Google Docs.

2. At the top of the document in the **Unsaved spreadsheet** box, type your last name and the title "Sources of Electricity." Click **OK** in the **Save Spreadsheet** window.

3. Spreadsheets are made up of columns that are identified by letters (A, B, C, etc.) and rows that are identified by numbers (1, 2, 3, etc.).

4. The location within a spreadsheet where a column meets a row is called a *cell* and is identified by both a letter and number (Figure 7-2).

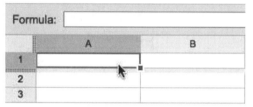

Figure 7-2

5. Click into cell **A1**, and type the label "Source."

6. Next, hit the **Tab** key on your keyboard. This will move you over into cell **B1**. Now type "Percentage."

7. Click and drag over cells **A1** and **B1** to highlight them. Use the **Align** button to center the labels in their cells and the **Bold** button (**B**) to make them bold (Figure 7-3).

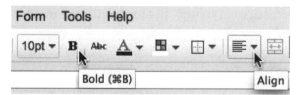

Figure 7-3

8. Next, click into cell **A2** and type "Hydroelectric." Now hit the **Tab** key on your keyboard. This will take you over to cell **B2**. Type **0.068**.

9. Use the following table to complete entering your data.

Source	Percentage
Hydroelectric	0.068
Coal	0.445
Natural Gas	0.233
Petroleum	0.01
Nuclear	0.202
Renewables	0.036
Other	0.006

Where Does Our Electricity Come From? *(cont.)*

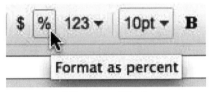

Spreadsheets

Activity 7

10. Once your data is entered, click and drag over both columns **A** and **B** to highlight them, and use the **Align** button to center the data in the cells.

11. Now you will change the format of the numbers in column B so they display as a percent. To do this, highlight the numbers by clicking and dragging over them.

12. Next, click the **Format as percent** button (Figure 7-4).

Figure 7-4

13. You can also change the format of numbers in a cell by clicking the **More formats** button (Figure 7-5).

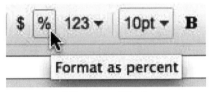

Figure 7-5

14. Now you are going to use the Sort function to arrange the sources of electricity from greatest to least. To do this, highlight the percentages in column B, then select the **Data** menu, and choose **Sort sheet by column B, Z-A** (Figure 7-6).

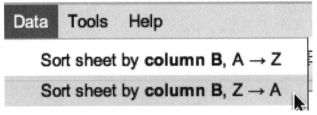

Figure 7-6

15. Next, click into cell **A1**, then go to the **Insert** menu and choose **Chart**. You can also click on the **Insert chart...** button (Figure 7-7).

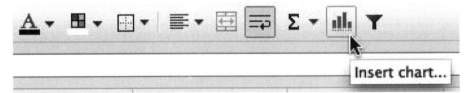

Figure 7-7

16. You will now use the **Chart Editor** window to create a pie chart. Make sure there is a check mark in the **Use row 1 as headers** box.

Activity 7

17. Next, go to the **Charts** tab, click on **Pie** and select **3d pie chart**, which is the option below **pie chart** (Figure 7-8).

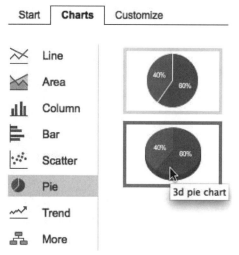

Figure 7-8

18. A preview of your chart will now appear in the **Preview** window. Now click on the **Customize** link.

19. In the **Customize** window, click in the **Chart title** box and type "Sources of Electricity in the U.S. 2009;" then click out of that box. The chart title should now appear above your chart. Next click on the **Name** link and change the name to "Pie Chart" (Figure 7-9).

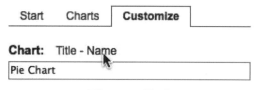

Figure 7-9

20. Next, under **Style**, you can select a specific series of data and change the color of its pie slice within the chart. For example, click on the drop-down menu, and select **Coal** (Figure 7-10).

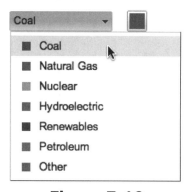

Figure 7-10

Activity 7

21. Change the color of coal's pie slice to gray by clicking on the color box and selecting the color gray (Figure 7-11).

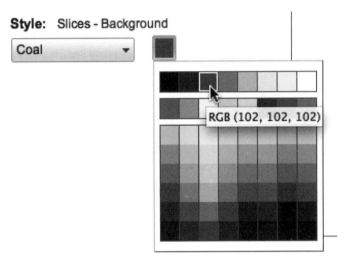

Figure 7-11

22. Now that your chart has been set up, click the **Insert** button located at the bottom-right corner of the **Chart Editor** window.

23. To display your chart as its own page within your spreadsheet, click on the chart and select the **Pie Chart** menu located in the upper left corner of the chart (Figure 7-12).

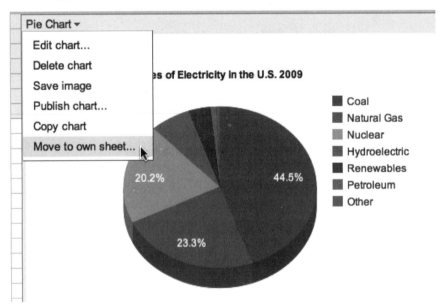

Figure 7-12

24 Under the **Pie Chart** menu, select the **Move to own sheet...** option. This will insert your chart on its own page. Try hovering over a pie slice with your cursor. It should produce a pop-up of the data for each pie slice. Your project is now complete!

U.S. Energy Sources

Activity 8

Objectives

Each student will utilize the Google Docs spreadsheet application to create a multiple-line chart showing the changes in major sources of energy in the United States.

Benchmarks for Technology Standards

Students will know the characteristics, uses, and basic features of computer software programs, including:

* knowing the common features and uses of spreadsheets
* using spreadsheet software to update, add, and delete data, and to produce charts

Learning Objectives

At the end of this lesson, students will be able to:

1. know the various terms associated with spreadsheets, including rows, columns, and cells

2. enter data into a spreadsheet

3. adjust the width of a selected column

4. change the alignment of data within a cell

5. change the style of data within a cell

6. use the Autofill function to automatically insert data into a column

7. create and format a multiple-line chart from data entered within a spreadsheet

Before the Computer

You might want to brief your students about the five different sources of energy used in this activity. Explain what they are, and how they are used to produce electricity. Also, this activity uses the energy unit known as a *quad*. One quad is equal to one quadrillion BTUs, or British Thermal Units. One BTU is equal to about the same amount of energy given off by one match. Inform your students that one quad is a very large number that has 15 zeros! Therefore, one quad of energy is equivalent to lighting one quadrillion matches! An example of a completed project is shown in Figure 8-1.

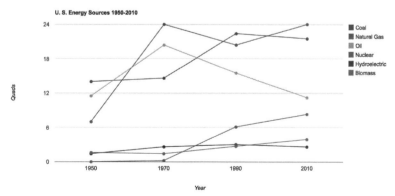

Figure 8-1

U.S. Energy Sources *(cont.)*

Activity 8

Procedure

1. Open a new spreadsheet document using Google Docs.

2. At the top of the document in the **Unsaved spreadsheet** box, type your last name and then "U.S. Energy Use." Click **OK** in the **Save Spreadsheet** window.

3. Spreadsheets are made up of columns that are identified by letters (A, B, C, etc.) and rows that are identified by numbers (1, 2, 3, etc.).

4. The location within a spreadsheet where a column meets a row is called a *cell*, and is identified by both a letter and number (Figure 8-2).

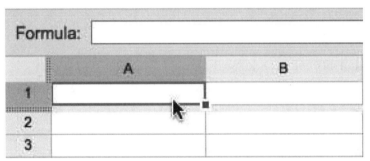

Figure 8-2

5. Click into cell **A1** and enter the following column label: "Year."

6. Hit the **Tab** key on your keyboard to move you over to the next cell and type "Coal."

7. Move into cell **C1** and type "Natural Gas."

8. In cell **D1**, enter "Oil," in cell **E1**: "Nuclear," cell **F1**: "Hydroelectric," and in cell **G1**, "Biomass."

9. Next, highlight all of the labels in row 1 by clicking and dragging over them, increase their font size to **12** by clicking the **Font size** button, and also use the **Bold** button (**B**) to make the font bold (Figure 8-3).

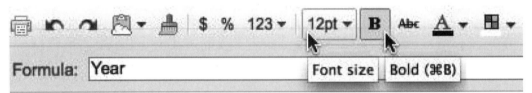

Figure 8-3

10. Now center your labels by using the **Align** button (Figure 8-4).

Figure 8-4

U.S. Energy Sources (cont.)

Activity 8

11. Click into cell **A2** and type "1950." Hit the **Enter** key on your keyboard to take you down to cell **A3** and type "1970."

12. Next, you are going to use the Autofill function to automatically fill in the remaining years in column A. Click and drag over cells **A2** and **A3** to highlight them.

13. With the cells still highlighted, move your cursor to the bottom-right corner of cell **A3** until the cursor changes into a cross (Figure 8-5).

2	1950
3	1970
4	

Figure 8-5

14. Now click and drag down column A until you get to cell **A5**. Your years should now be automatically filled in up to 2010.

15. Next, use the data below to fill out the rest of your spreadsheet.

Year	Coal	Natural Gas	Oil	Nuclear	Hydroelectric	Biomass
1950	14	7	11.5	0	1.4	1.6
1970	14.6	24	20.4	0.2	2.6	1.4
1990	22.4	20.4	15.5	6.1	3	2.7
2010	21.5	24	11.2	8.3	2.6	3.9

16. Once your data is entered, highlight it by clicking and dragging over it, then center it using the **Align** button.

17. With all of your data highlighted, change the font size to **12 pt** using the **Font size** button.

18. Next, you are going to use your data to make a line chart. Click into cell **A1**, then go to the **Insert** menu and choose **Chart**, or you can hit the **Insert chart...** button (Figure 8-6).

Figure 8-6

Spreadsheets

19. You will now use the **Chart Editor** window to create a line chart. Make sure there is a check mark in the **Use row 1 as headers** box, then put a check mark in the **Use column A as labels** box. Now click the **Charts** link (Figure 8-7).

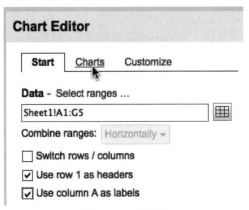

Figure 8-7

20. Next, under the **Charts** tab, click on **Line** and select **line chart**, which is the option above **smooth line chart** (Figure 8-8).

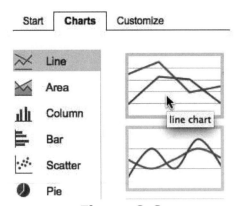

Figure 8-8

21. A preview of your chart will now appear in the Preview window. Now click on the Customize link (Figure 8-9).

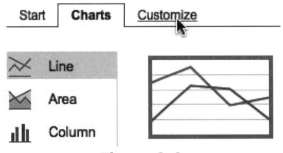

Figure 8-9

22. In the **Customize** window, click in the **Chart Title** box and type "U.S. Energy Sources 1950–2010." Click out of the box. The chart title should now appear above your chart. Next, click on the **Name** link.

23. This will give your chart a name that is linked to your spreadsheet data. Type the following in the Chart Name box: "Line Chart."

24. Now click into the **Axis: Vertical** box and type the name of your vertical axis, which is "Quads." Next, click the **Horizontal** axis link. (Figure 8-10).

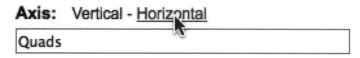

Figure 8-10

25. In the **Horizontal** axis box, type the label "Year."

26. Next, under **Style** click the **Point** link (Figure 8-11).

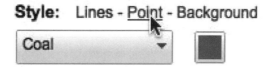

Figure 8-11

27. Under the **Point** drop-down menu, choose **Medium**.

28. Now that your chart is set up, click the **Insert** button located at the bottom-right corner of the **Chart Editor** window.

29. To display your chart as its own page within your spreadsheet, click on the chart and select the **Line Chart** menu located in the upper-left corner of the chart.

30. Under the **Line Chart** drop-down menu, select the **Move to own sheet...** option. This will insert your chart on its own page. Your project is now complete!

Phases of the Moon

Activity 9

Drawing

Objectives

Each student will utilize the Google Docs drawing application to create a diagram that shows the eight phases of the moon in a month.

Benchmarks for Technology Standards

Students will know the characteristics, uses, and basic features of computer software programs, including:

- the common features and uses of desktop publishing and word-processing software
- knowing that documents can be created, designed, and formatted
- importing images into a document

Learning Objectives

At the end of this lesson, students will be able to:

1. use the shape tool to create a circle
2. change the fill and line color of a shape
3. rotate a shape within a drawing
4. label a shape using the Text box tool
5. change the size and style of font within a text box
6. copy and paste objects within a drawing
7. change the background color of a drawing

Variations

This activity was written using the eight phases of the moon for the month of May in the year 2011. You can adapt it easily to display the phases of the moon for a specific month by going to the following website: **http://stardate.org/nightsky/moon**. Just substitute the correct date for each moon phase for the month you want to use. An example of a completed project is shown in Figure 9-1.

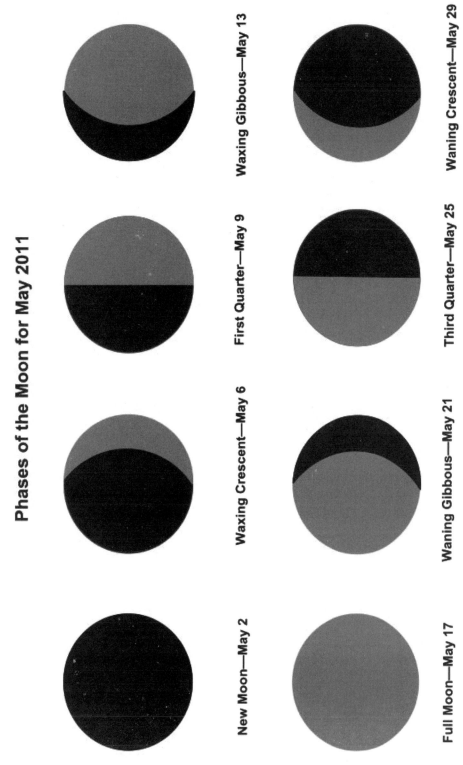

Phases of the Moon for May 2011

Waxing Gibbous—May 13

Waning Crescent—May 29

First Quarter—May 9

Third Quarter—May 25

Waxing Crescent—May 6

Waning Gibbous—May 21

New Moon—May 2

Full Moon—May 17

Figure 9-1

Phases of the Moon *(cont.)*

Activity 9

Procedure

1. Open a new drawing document in Google Docs.
2. At the top of the document in the **Untitled drawing** box, type your last name and then the title "Moon Phases." Click **OK** in the **Rename Document** window.
3. Click on the **Shape** tool, select **Shapes**, and choose **Oval** (Figure 9-2).

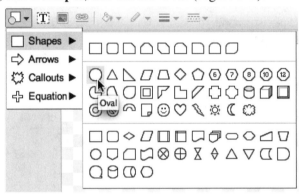

Figure 9-2

4. Next, move your cursor to the upper-left corner of your page. Leave some room at the top of the page for the title you will be adding later. While pressing and holding the **Shift** button on your keyboard, click and drag down toward the right to draw a circle about the size of a quarter, then let go of your mouse and the shift button. (Figure 9-3).

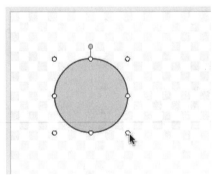

Figure 9-3

5. The circle you drew is known as an object within a drawing. When you click on an object to select it, its anchor points show. With your circle selected, click the **Fill color** button and change the fill color of your circle to **black** (Figure 9-4).

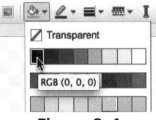

Figure 9-4

6. With your circle still selected, click the **Line color** button and change the line color to **black** (Figure 9-5).

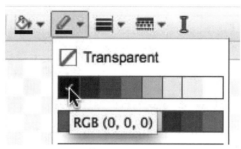

Figure 9-5

7. Next, you will copy and paste your circle. Right-click on the circle (or control-click if you are using a Macintosh computer), and choose **Copy** (Figure 9-6).

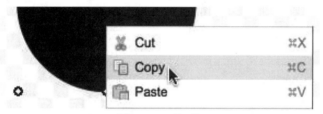

Figure 9-6

8. Now move your cursor just to the right of your circle, right-click (or control-click), and choose **Paste**. You may have to move your newly pasted circle by clicking and dragging it to the right.

9. Repeat these steps again until you have eight circles in two rows of four (Figure 9-7).

Figure 9-7

Drawing

10. Next, click on the **Text box** button (Figure 9-8).

Figure 9-8

11. Move your cursor below the first circle, then click and drag to form a small rectangle (Figure 9-9).

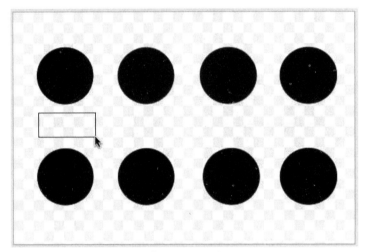

Figure 9-9

12. In the text box window, type "New Moon—May 2" (Figure 9-10).

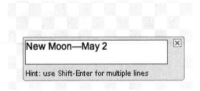

Figure 9-10

13. Hit the **Enter** key on your keyboard. Now click the **Bold** button and also change the font size to **12** by clicking the **Font size** button (Figure 9-11).

Figure 9-11

Phases of the Moon *(cont.)*

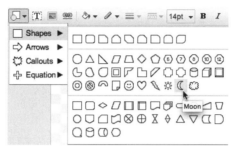

Activity 9

14. Next, click the **Shape** button, select **Shapes**, and choose the **Moon** shape (Figure 9-12).

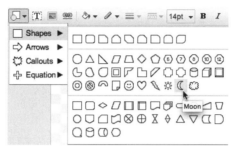

Figure 9-12

15. Move your cursor to the top of the second circle, and then click and drag down to make a crescent shape that fits on the left side of the circle (Figure 9-13).

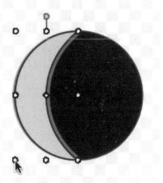

Figure 9-13

16. Next, change the fill color and line color of the crescent to gray.

17. Now take your cursor and click on the anchor point near the top of the crescent. Drag the object clockwise until you have rotated it 180 degrees (Figure 9-14).

Figure 9-14

18. Click and drag the crescent to the right so it fits within the black circle. Use the **Text box** tool to label this phase "Waxing Crescent—May 6." Reduce the font size of the text to **12** and make it **bold**.

Phases of the Moon *(cont.)*

Activity 9

19. Next, click the **Shape** button, select **Shapes**, and choose **Pie** (Figure 9-15).

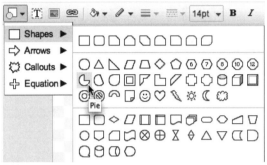

Figure 9-15

20. Place your cursor in the middle of the third circle of the top row. Click and drag up to the top of the circle (Figure 9-16), then let go of the mouse button and rotate your cursor clockwise until the right half of the circle is covered (Figure 9-17). Click your mouse again.

Figure 9-16

Figure 9-17

21. Your circle should now be half covered. Change the fill and line colors to gray (Figure 9-18).

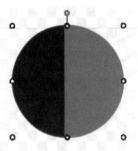

Figure 9-18

22. Use the **Text box** tool to add the following text below the shape: "First Quarter—May 9." Make the title **bold** and the font size **12**.

23. Click on the last circle in the top row and change its fill and line colors to gray. Then select the **Moon** shape from **Shapes** under the **Shape** menu, and click and draw a crescent shape that covers the left part of the circle (Figure 9-19).

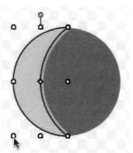

Figure 9-19

24. Change the fill and line colors of this crescent shape to black. Then add a text box that reads "Waxing Gibbous—May 13." Make the text **bold** and the font size **12**.

25. Next, click on the circle located at the bottom-right corner of the page and change its fill and line colors to gray.

25. Add a text box below it that reads "Full Moon—May 17." Make the label **bold** and the font size **12**.

27. Click on the next circle and change its line and fill colors to gray. Then use the **Moon** shape tool to draw a crescent shape. Change the crescent's fill and line colors to black, then click on its anchor point and rotate the crescent 180 degrees clockwise (Figure 9-20).

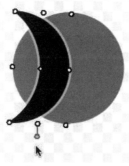

Figure 9-20

28. Move the crescent to cover the right side of the circle. Use the Text box tool to label this phase "Waning Gibbous—May 21."

29. Use Figure 9-21 below to complete the last two phases of the moon.

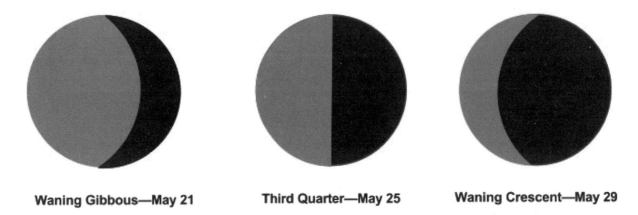

Waning Gibbous—May 21   Third Quarter—May 25   Waning Crescent—May 29

Figure 9-21

30. Once you have completed the final two phases and added their labels, draw a text box at the top of your drawing. Type the following title for your drawing: "Phases of the Moon for May 2011." Increase the font size to **18** and make it **bold**.

31. Finally, go to the **Format** menu and choose **Background**. Change the color of the background to white.

32. Your project is complete!

English and Metric Rulers

Activity 10

Objectives

Each student will utilize the Google Docs drawing application to create a diagram that shows the basic measurements used on both English and Metric system rulers.

Benchmarks for Technology Standards

Students will know the characteristics, uses, and basic features of computer software programs, including:

- using the common features of desktop publishing and word-processing software
- knowing that documents can be created, designed, and formatted

Learning Objectives

At the end of this lesson, students will be able to:

1. use the Shape tool to create rectangles.
2. change the fill and line color of a shape
3. use the line tool to create lines
4. change the thickness and color of a line
5. label a shape using the Text box tool
6. change the size and style of font within a text box
7. group objects in a drawing
8. use the Word Art tool
9. change the fill and line color of Word Art

Before the Computer

An example of a completed project is shown in Figure 10-1.

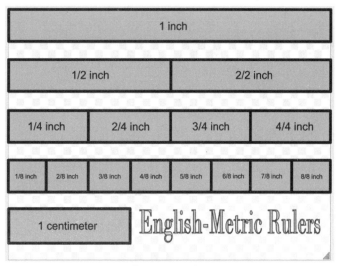

Figure 10-1

English and Metric Rulers *(cont.)*

Activity 10

Procedure

1. Open a new drawing document in Google Docs.

2. At the top of the document in the **Untitled drawing** box, type your last name and then the title "Rulers." Click **OK** in the **Rename Document** window.

3. Click on the **Shape** tool, select **Shapes**, and choose **Rectangle** (Figure 10-2).

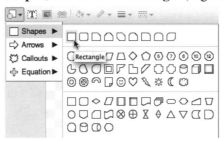

Figure 10-2

4. Take your cursor to the very top-right corner of the drawing page and click and drag down four grid squares, and continue to drag across the page to the edge to draw a large rectangle (Figure 10-3).

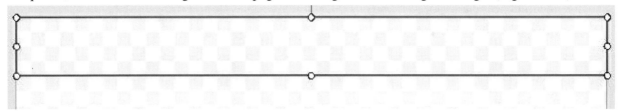

Figure 10-3

5. With your rectangle still highlighted, click the **Fill color** button and change the color of the fill to **gray** (Figure 10-4).

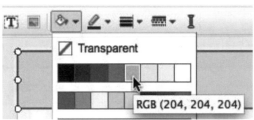

Figure 10-4

6. Next, with the rectangle still highlighted, use the **Line width** tool to increase the thickness of the rectangle's border to **8px** (Figure 10-5).

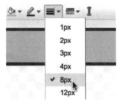

Figure 10-5

English and Metric Rulers *(cont.)*

Activity 10

7. Next, change the line color to black using the **Line color** button (Figure 10-6).

Figure 10-6

8. Next, select the **Text box** tool (Figure 10-7).

Figure 10-7

9. Click and drag your cursor to draw a text box in the center of the rectangle. Type the following label: "1 inch" (Figure 10-8).

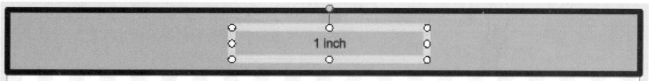

Figure 10-8

10. Next, increase the font size of the text to **24pt** by using the **Font size** button (Figure 10-9).

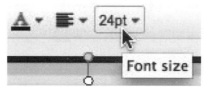

Figure 10-9

11. Now click on your rectangle to highlight it. Go to the **Edit** menu and choose **Copy**. Then choose **Paste** from the **Edit** menu to insert a copy of your rectangle. You can also right-click (or control-click) on an object and select **Copy**. Drag the new rectangle to just below the first one (Figure 10-10).

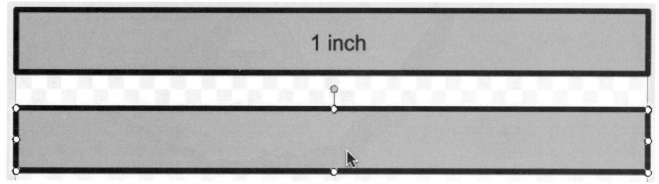

Figure 10-10

English and Metric Rulers *(cont.)*

Activity 10

12. Now click the **Line** button (Figure 10-11).

Figure 10-11

13. Move your cursor over to the top center of your rectangle. Indicators should pop up to reveal the center of the rectangle. Click and drag your cursor down to draw a line between the dots that divide the rectangle in half (Figure 10-12).

Figure 10-12

14. Use the **Line width** tool to increase the size of the line to **8px**.

15. Now you are going to combine the line with your rectangle using the Group function. Click the **Select** tool (Figure 10-13).

Figure 10-13

16. While holding down the **Shift** key on your keyboard, click and highlight the rectangle and the line. They should now be highlighted. Let go of the **Shift** key. Go to the **Arrange** menu and choose **Group** (Figure 10-14).

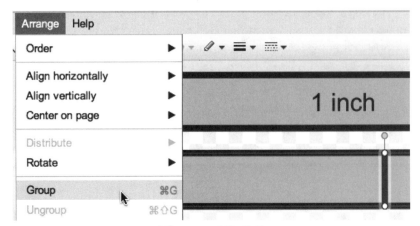

Figure 10-14

17. Your objects will now be grouped together as one object whenever they are selected.

18. Next, draw a text box in the middle of the left half of the rectangle and type, "1/2 inch" (Figure 10-15).

Figure 10-15

19. Increase its font size to **24**, then draw another text box in the right half of the rectangle and type "2/2 inch." Change the size to **24**.

20. Next, right-click or control-click on the second rectangle and choose **Copy**, then **Paste**. Drag the new rectangle just below the second one. Select the **Line** tool and draw two new lines that divide the halves of the rectangle (Figure 10-16). Pressing and holding the **Shift** key will help make straight lines. Change the color of the new lines to black, and increase their width to **8px**.

Figure 10-16

21. Next, use the **Select** tool to highlight the new lines and the rectangle. Then use the **Group** function to combine them into one object.

22. Now use the **Text Box** tool to draw four labels in each section of the rectangle as shown in Figure 10-17. Set the font size to **24**.

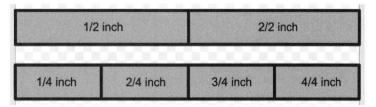

Figure 10-17

23. Right-click or control-click on the third rectangle and choose **Copy** and **Paste**. Drag the new rectangle to just below the third one. Use the line tool to draw lines **8px** in thickness that will divide the quarters in half (Figure 10-18).

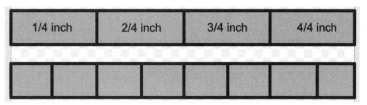

Figure 10-18

24. Insert a text box to label each section as shown in Figure 10-19. Select a font size of **14**.

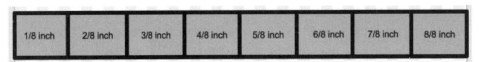

| 1/8 inch | 2/8 inch | 3/8 inch | 4/8 inch | 5/8 inch | 6/8 inch | 7/8 inch | 8/8 inch |

Figure 10-19

25. Next, use the **Shape** tool to draw one final rectangle that is about 3/8 as long as the rectangle above it (Figure 10-20).

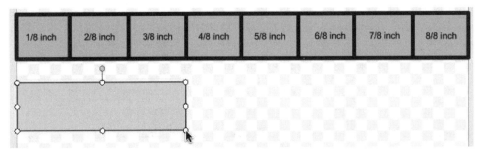

Figure 10-20

26. Change the fill color to gray and the line color to black. Also increase the width of the line to **8px**.

27. Use the **Text box** tool to label this rectangle "1 centimeter" (Figure 10-21). Increase its font size to **24**.

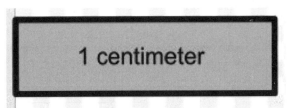
1 centimeter

Figure 10-21

28. Now you will create a title for your drawing using the **Word Art** tool. Click on the **Insert** menu and select **Word Art** (Figure 10-22).

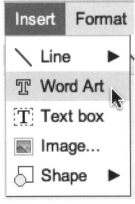

| Insert | Format |

- ＼ Line ▶
- 𝕋 Word Art
- T Text box
- ▣ Image…
- ⬠ Shape ▶

Figure 10-22

29. Type the following into the Word Art box: "English-Metric Rulers." Hit the **Enter** key on your keyboard. Now click and drag the word art box down to the blank space next to the 1 centimeter box. Click and drag the anchor points to make the word art box fit within the space (Figure 10-23).

Figure 10-23

30. Finally, with the Word Art box still highlighted, go to the **Font** menu and change the Word Art font to **Bodoni** (Figure 10-24).

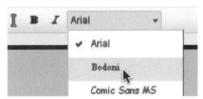

Figure 10-24

31. You can also change the fill and line colors of the Word Art using the **Fill color** and **Line color** buttons. Your project is now complete!

Time Zones

Activity 11

~~~~~~

Objectives

Each student will utilize the Google Docs drawing application to create a diagram that shows the four time zones within the continental United States, plus time zones in Alaska and Hawaii.

Benchmarks for Technology Standards

Students will know the characteristics, uses, and basic features of computer software programs, including:

- knowing the common features and uses of desktop publishing and word-processing software
- knowing that documents can be created, designed, and formatted

Learning Objectives

At the end of this lesson, students will be able to:

1. insert an image into a drawing document
2. use the Polyline tool to create irregular shapes
3. change the fill and line color of a shape
4. use the Arrow tool to create lines with arrowheads
5. change the thickness and color of a line
6. label a shape using the Text box tool
7. change the size and style of font within a text box

Before the Computer

This activity requires the use of a map image of the United States, which needs to be saved in a location for students to access. You can download a free version from the following website, **http://www.worldatlas.com/webimage/testmaps/usanames.htm**. Save the image file in a shared class folder before beginning this lesson. You may also wish to instruct your students to go to the above website and save the image on their computers before beginning the activity. An example of a completed project is shown in Figure 11-1.

Figure 11-1

Time Zones (cont.)

Activity 11

Procedure

1. Open a new drawing document in Google Docs.

2. At the top of the document in the **Untitled drawing** box, type your last name and then the title "Time Zones." Click **OK** in the **Rename Document** window.

3. Click on the **Insert** menu and choose **Image**. Click on **Upload**, then click the **Choose File** button (Figure 11-2).

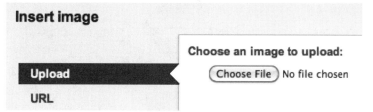

Figure 11-2

4. Navigate to the map file on your computer. Click **Open**. The image should now appear in your drawing. Grab the bottom-right anchor point and drag it to enlarge the map until it fills about ¾ of your page (Figure 11-3).

Figure 11-3

5. Next, click the **Polyline** tool (Figure 11-4). If the Polyline tool does not appear on your toolbar, you can add it by going to the **Insert** menu, selecting **Line**, and choosing **Polyline**.

Figure 11-4

Time Zones *(cont.)*

Activity 11

6. The Polyline tool allows you to draw an irregularly shaped object made up of straight lines. Bring your cursor to the top of the state of Maine. Click once, then move your cursor down to the top of New Hampshire, then click once again. You should have drawn a line (Figure 11-5).

Figure 11-5

7. Every time you click, you can extend your line until you eventually return to where you started. Then you double-click to create a multi-sided object called a polygon. Now continue to roughly trace the outline of the border of the northern states until you get to the top of Wisconsin where it meets the Michigan border (Figure 11-6).

Figure 11-6

8. Now continue your line down the eastern borders of Wisconsin and Illinois, then cut across Kentucky, Tennessee, the border between Georgia and Alabama, and finally down through the Florida Panhandle (Figure 11-7).

Figure 11-7

Time Zones *(cont.)*

Activity 11

9. Next, continue to follow down and around the coast of Florida, then up the east coast until you return to your starting point. Then double-click and your polygon will be created (Figure 11-8).

Figure 11-8

10. Next, you will remove the fill of your polygon in order to make it transparent. Click the **Fill color** button and choose **Transparent** (Figure 11-9).

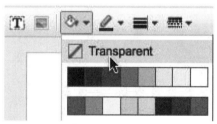

Figure 11-9

11. Now click the **Line width** button and change the thickness of your polygon's line to **12px** (Figure 11-10).

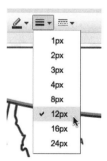

Figure 11-10

12. Next, click the **Line color** button and choose **dark green** (Figure 11-11).

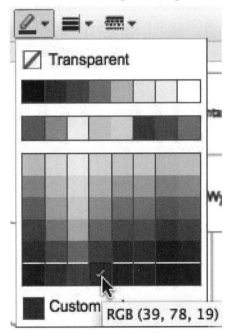

Figure 11-11

13. Now choose the **Polyline** tool again and place your cursor at the top of the map between Montana and North Dakota. Trace the next time zone as shown in Figure 11-12.

Figure 11-12

14. Next, change the fill of your second polygon to **Transparent**, the line color to **blue**, and its line width to **12px**.

15. Now choose the **Polyline** tool again and trace the next time zone as shown in Figure 11-13.

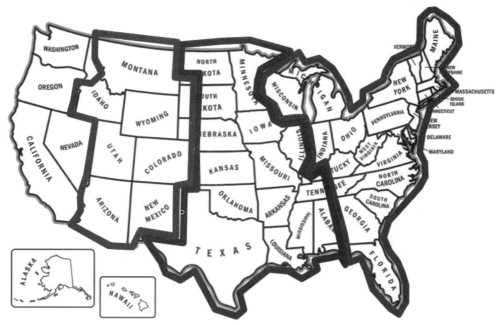

Figure 11-13

16. Next, change the fill of your third polygon to **Transparent**, the line color to **red**, and its line width to **12px**.

17. Now, starting at the northwestern tip of Washington state, use the **Polyline** tool to trace down along the west coast and back up through the eastern borders of Nevada, Oregon, and Washington to form your fourth time zone (Figure 11-14).

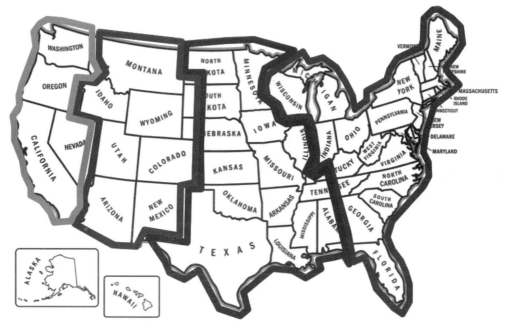

Figure 11-14

18. Next, change the fill of your fourth polygon to **Transparent**, the line color to **orange**, and its line width to **12px**.

19. Now use your **Polyline** tool to draw a polygon around Alaska. Then change its fill to **Transparent**, the line color to **yellow**, and its line width to **12px** (Figure 11-15).

Figure 11-15

20. Next, draw one final polygon around Hawaii. Make its fill **Transparent**, its line width **12px**, and its color **aqua blue**.

21. Now that you have drawn all of your time zones, you will label them. Click on the **Text box** button (Figure 11-16).

Figure 11-16

22. Use the **Text box** tool to draw a rectangle just to the right of the tip of Florida. Then type "Eastern Time 11:00 AM" and hit the **Enter** key on your keyboard (Figure 11-17).

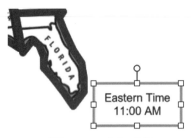

Figure 11-17

23. With the text box still highlighted, click the **Bold** button to make the text **bold** (Figure 11-18).

Figure 11-18

Time Zones (cont.)

Activity 11

24. With the text box still highlighted, change its line color to the same green as the polygon by using the **Line color** button. Also change the thickness of the line to **12px** using the **Line width** button.

25. Next, you are going to draw an arrow connecting the text box to the time zone. To do this, click the **Arrow** tool (Figure 11-19). If the Arrow tool does not appear in your toolbar, you can add it by going to the **Insert** menu, selecting **Line**, and choosing **Arrow**.

Figure 11-19

26. Now click and drag from the text box to the coast of South Carolina (Figure 11-20). With the arrow still highlighted, change its color to **green** using the **Line color** button and increase its thickness to **4px** using the **Line width** button.

Figure 11-20

27. Next, draw five textboxes for the remaining time zones as shown in Figure 11-21. Change the line color of each text box and its arrow to match its time zone. Also increase the width of the arrow to **4px** and the line around the textbox to **12px** using the **Line width** tool.

Figure 11-21

28. Finally, use the **Text box** tool to add the following title to the bottom of your drawing: "Time Zones of the U.S." Your project is complete!

Class Survey

Activity 12

~~~~~~

Objectives

Each student will utilize the Google Docs form application to create a simple survey that gathers information about his or her classmates. Each member of the class will take the survey. Each student will then analyze his or her results.

Benchmarks for Technology Standards

Students will know the characteristics, uses, and basic features of computer software programs, including:

- using the common features and uses of desktop publishing and word processing software
- knowing that documents can be created, designed, and formatted

Learning Objectives

At the end of this lesson, students will be able to:

1. create a new form
2. add a title and instructions to a form
3. insert a text question into a form
4. format a text question within a form
5. format a checkbox question within a form
6. email a form to a group
7. view the results of a form

Before the Computer

The use of forms in Google Docs requires students to email one another to get responses to the questions in their forms. Before beginning this activity, you should prepare a document to share with the class that has all of your students' email addresses. It usually is best to provide them with a file that contains the addresses so they can just copy and paste them when needed. This alleviates any spelling mistakes that can disrupt the process. An example form for this activity is shown in Figure 12-1.

Forms

Class Survey *(cont.)*

Activity 12

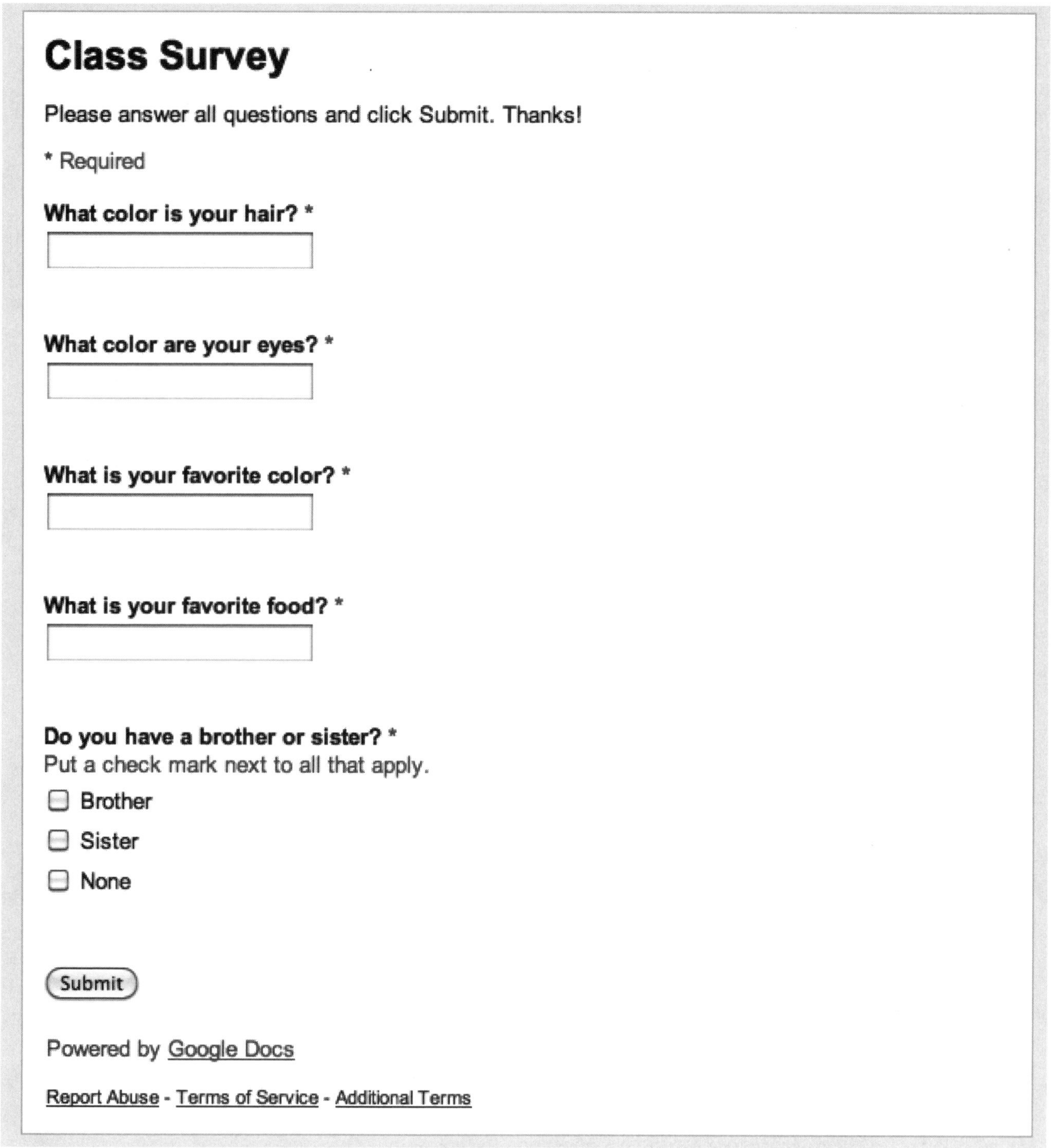

Class Survey

Please answer all questions and click Submit. Thanks!

* Required

What color is your hair? *

What color are your eyes? *

What is your favorite color? *

What is your favorite food? *

Do you have a brother or sister? *
Put a check mark next to all that apply.

- Brother
- Sister
- None

Submit

Powered by Google Docs

Report Abuse - Terms of Service - Additional Terms

Figure 12-1

Class Survey *(cont.)*

Activity 12

Procedure

1. Open a new form document in Google Docs.

2. At the top of the document in the **Untitled form** box, type your last name and the title "Class Survey."

3. In the box below your form's title, type the following directions: "Please answer all questions and click Submit. Thanks!"

4. Below the directions box is your first question. Click into the **Question Title** box and type your first question, "What color is your hair?" (Figure 12-2).

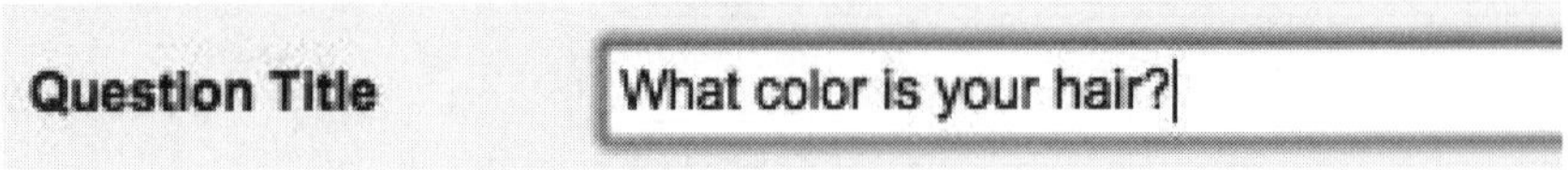

Figure 12-2

5. Next, put a check mark in the box next to **Make this a required question** and then click **Done**.

6. Move your cursor down to Question 2. It should turn a shade of yellow and bring up three icons near the right side of the page.

7. Click on the **Edit** icon, which looks like a pencil (Figure 12-3).

Figure 12-3

8. Click into the **Question Title** box and type your next question, "What color are your eyes?"

9. Put a check mark in the box next to **Make this a required question** and then click **Done**.

10. Next, click on the **Duplicate** icon (Figure 12-4). This will insert another question that is exactly like the previous question into your form.

Figure 12-4

11. Now replace the text in the box with your next question, "What is your favorite color?"

12. Put a check mark in the box next to **Make this a required question** and then click **Done**.

13. Click the **Duplicate** icon to create another question: "What is your favorite food?"

Class Survey *(cont.)*
Activity 12

14. Finally, insert one more question. This time you are going to make it a question that includes checkboxes for answers.

15. In the Question Title box, type "Do you have a brother or sister?"

16. In the **Help Text** box, type "Put a check mark next to all that apply."

17. Next, click on the **Question Type** drop down menu and choose the **Checkboxes** option (Figure 12-5).

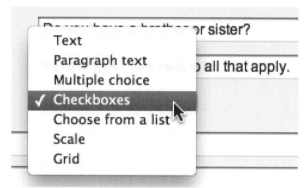

Figure 12-5

18. Click into the **Option 1** box and type "Brother." Then hit the **Enter** key on your keyboard to create an **Option 2** box (Figure 12-6).

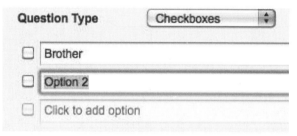

Figure 12-6

19. Type "Sister" in the **Option 2** box, then click into the **Click to add option box** and type "None."

20. Put a check mark in the box next to **Make this a required question** and click **Done**. Your questionnaire is now complete.

21. Next, you will make a list of email addresses to which you will send your questionnaire. Click on the **Email this form** button at the top of your form (Figure 12-7).

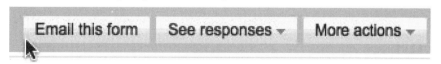

Figure 12-7

22. In the **Send this form to others** window, enter the email addresses of your classmates that were provided by your teacher. Then click **Send**.

23. Your form will now be emailed to your classmates. You can click on the **See responses** button to view the results. Your project is now complete!

Pet Survey

Activity 13

Objectives

Each student will utilize the Google Docs form application to create a survey about the pets that his or her classmates have. Each student will then analyze the results.

Benchmarks for Technology Standards

Students will know the characteristics, uses, and basic features of computer software programs, including:

- using the common features of desktop publishing and word processing software
- knowing that documents can be created, designed, and formatted

Learning Objectives

At the end of this lesson, students will be able to:

1. create a new form
2. add a title and instructions to a form
3. insert a text question into a form
4. format a text question within a form
5. format a choose-from-list question within a form
6. format a scale question within a form
7. email a form to a group
8. view the results of a form

Before the Computer

The use of forms in Google Docs requires students to email one another to get responses to their forms. Before beginning this activity, you should prepare a document to share with the class that has all of your students' email addresses. It usually is best to provide them with a file that contains the email addresses so they can just copy and paste them when needed. This alleviates any spelling mistakes that can disrupt the process. An example form for this activity is shown in Figure 13-1.

Pet Survey (cont.)

Activity 13

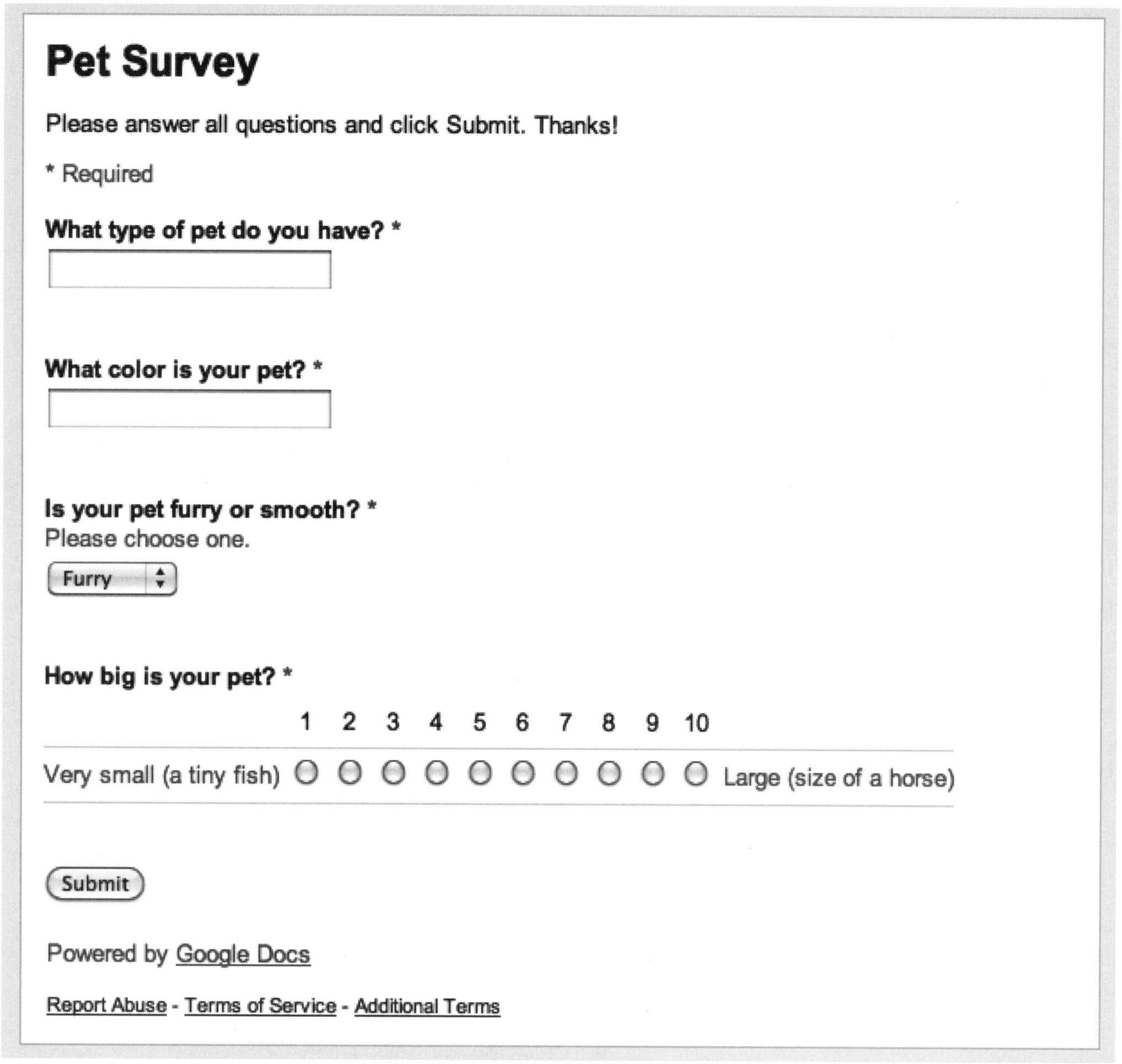

Pet Survey

Please answer all questions and click Submit. Thanks!

* Required

What type of pet do you have? *

What color is your pet? *

Is your pet furry or smooth? *
Please choose one.

Furry ▲▼

How big is your pet? *

	1	2	3	4	5	6	7	8	9	10	
Very small (a tiny fish)	○	○	○	○	○	○	○	○	○	○	Large (size of a horse)

Submit

Powered by Google Docs

Report Abuse - Terms of Service - Additional Terms

Figure 13-1

Pet Survey *(cont.)*
Activity 13

Procedure

1. Open a new form document in Google Docs.

2. At the top of the document in the **Untitled form** box, type your last name and the title "Pet Survey."

3. In the box below your form's title, type the following directions: "Please answer all questions and click Submit. Thanks!"

4. Below the directions box is your first question. Click into the **Question Title** box and type your first question, "What type of pet do you have?" (Figure 13-2).

Question Title	What type of pet do you have?

Figure 13-2

5. Next, put a check mark in the box next to **Make this a required question**.

6. Move your cursor down to Question 2. It should turn a shade of yellow and bring up three icons near the right side of the page.

7. Click on the **Edit** icon, which looks like a pencil (Figure 13-3).

Figure 13-3

8. Click into the **Question Title** box and type your next question, "What color is your pet?"

9. Put a check mark in the box next to **Make this a required question**, then click **Done**.

10. Next, click the **Add Item** button at the top-left corner of the page (Figure 13-4) and select **Text** to add another question.

Figure 13-4

11. You can also click on the **Duplicate** icon (Figure 13-5). This will insert a question that is exactly like the previous question into your form.

Figure 13-5

12. Now type your next question in the **Question Title** box: "Is your pet furry or smooth?"

13. In the **Help Text** box, type "Please choose one."

Forms

14. Next, click on the **Question Type** drop-down menu and choose the **Choose from a list** option (Figure 13-6).

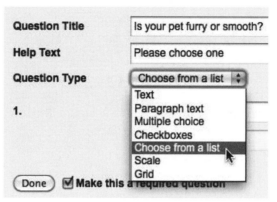

Figure 13-6

15. Click into the **Option 1** box and type "Furry." Then hit the **Enter** key on your keyboard to create an **Option 2** box (Figure 13-7).

Figure 13-7

16. Type "Smooth" in the **Option 2** box. Put a check mark in the box next to **Make this a required question**, then click **Done.**

17. Add a third question to your form and type "How big is your pet?" in the **Question Title** box.

18. This time you are going to set up a scale question. Choose **Scale** from the **Question Type** drop-down menu (Figure 13-8).

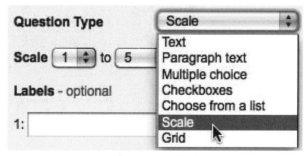

Figure 13-8

Pet Survey *(cont.)*

Activity 13

19. Now you must set the scale to use to answer this question. Set the scale from **1** to **10** using the drop down menus (Figure 13-9).

Figure 13-9

20. Now type a description of the scale. Under the **Labels** option in the first box, type "Very Small (a tiny fish)."

21. In the second box, type "Large (size of a horse)" (Figure 13-10).

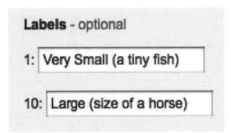

Figure 13-10

22. Put a check mark in the **Make this a required question** box. Your form is now complete. Click the **Done** button.

23. Next, you will make a list of email addresses to which you will send your questionnaire. Click on the **Email this form** button at the top of your form (Figure 13-11).

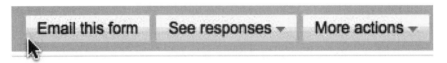

Figure 13-11

24. In the **Send this form to others** window, enter the email addresses of your classmates provided by your teacher. Then click **Send**.

25. Your form will now be emailed to your classmates. You can click on the **See responses** button to view the results. Your project is now complete!

Favorite Foods Survey

Activity 14

Objectives

Each student will utilize the Google Docs form application to create a survey about his or her classmates' favorite foods. He or she will then analyze the results.

Benchmarks for Technology Standards

Students will know the characteristics, uses, and basic features of computer software programs, including:

- using the common features of desktop publishing and word processing software
- knowing that documents can be created, designed, and formatted

Learning Objectives

At the end of this lesson, students will be able to:

1. create a new form
2. add a title and instructions to a form
3. insert a text question into a form
4. format a text question within a form
5. format a choose-from-list question within a form
6. format a scale question within a form
7. format a multiple-choice question
8. format a checkboxes question in a form
9. change the theme of a form
10. email a form to a group
11. view the results of your form

Before the Computer

The use of forms in Google Docs requires students to email one another to get responses to their forms. Before beginning this activity, you should prepare a document to share with the class that has all of your students' email addresses. It usually is best to provide them with a file that contains the email addresses so they can just copy and paste them when needed. This alleviates any spelling mistakes that can disrupt the process. An example form for this activity is shown in Figure 14-1.

Favorite Foods Survey *(cont.)*

Activity 14

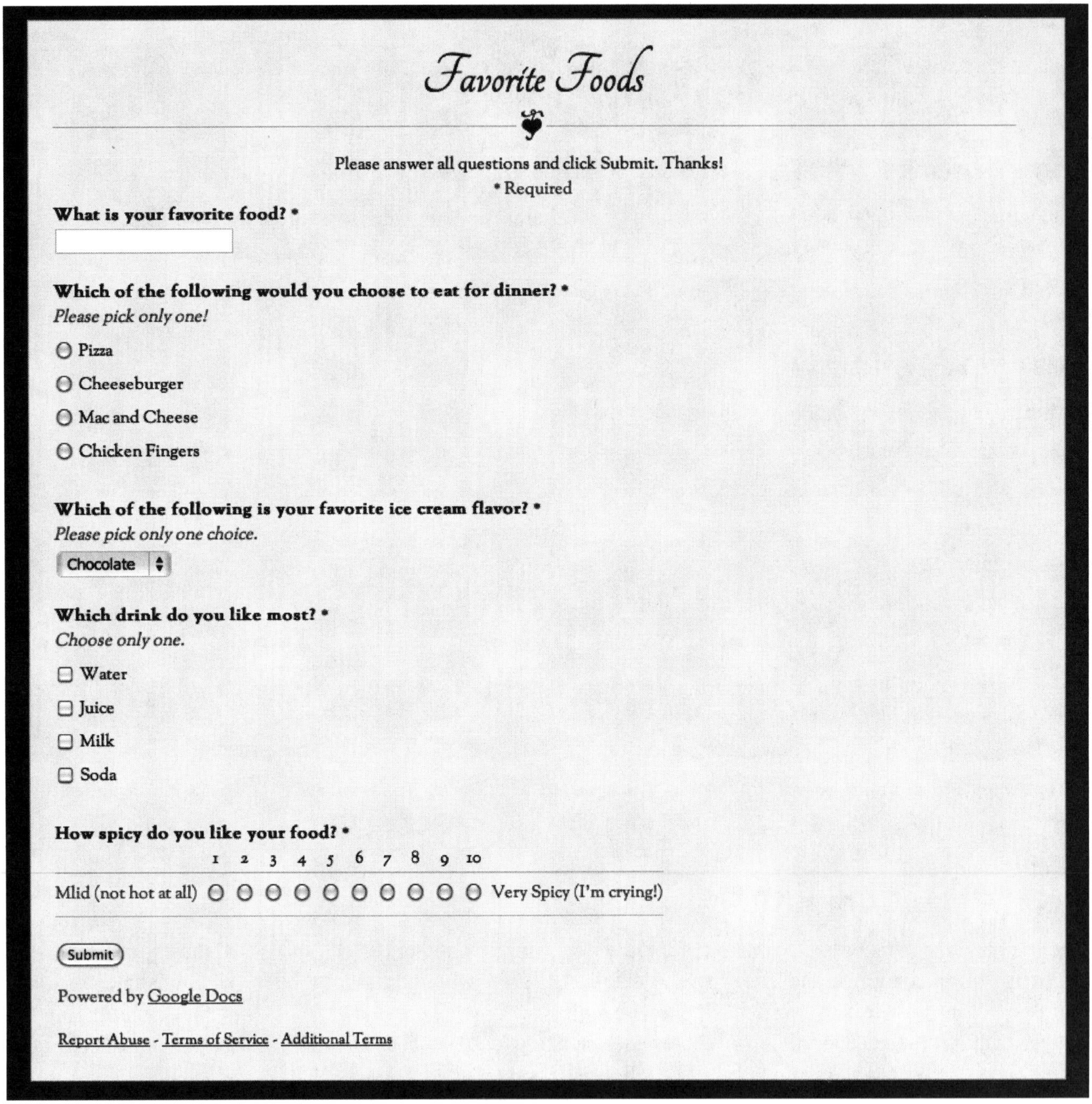

Favorite Foods

Please answer all questions and click Submit. Thanks!

* Required

What is your favorite food? *

Which of the following would you choose to eat for dinner? *

Please pick only one!

- Pizza
- Cheeseburger
- Mac and Cheese
- Chicken Fingers

Which of the following is your favorite ice cream flavor? *

Please pick only one choice.

Chocolate

Which drink do you like most? *

Choose only one.

- Water
- Juice
- Milk
- Soda

How spicy do you like your food? *

	1	2	3	4	5	6	7	8	9	10	
Mlid (not hot at all)	○	○	○	○	○	○	○	○	○	○	Very Spicy (I'm crying!)

Submit

Powered by Google Docs

Report Abuse - Terms of Service - Additional Terms

Figure 14-1

Favorite Foods Survey *(cont.)*

Activity 14

Procedure

1. Open a new form document in Google Docs.

2. At the top of the document in the **Untitled form** box, type your last name and the title "Favorite Foods."

3. In the box below your form's title, type the following directions: "Please answer all questions and click Submit. Thanks!"

4. Below the directions box is your first question. Click into the **Question Title** box and type your first question, "What is your favorite food?" (Figure 14-2).

Figure 14-2

5. Next, put a check mark in the box next to **Make this a required question**.

6. Move your cursor down to Question 2. It should turn a shade of yellow and bring up three icons near the right side of the page.

7. Click on the **Edit** icon, which looks like a pencil (Figure 14-3).

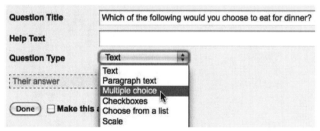

Figure 14-3

8. Next, you are going to create a multiple-choice question. Click into the **Question Title** box and type your next question, "Which of the following would you choose to eat for dinner?"

9. Next, click on the **Question Type** drop-down menu and choose the **Multiple choice** option (Figure 14-4).

Figure 14-4

10. In the **Help Text** box, type "Please pick only one!"

11. Next, you will enter the first choice in the **Option 1** box: "Pizza."

12. Click in the **Option 2** box and type "Cheeseburger." To add a third option, click in the **Click to add option** box (Figure 14-5).

Figure 14-5

13. Type "Mac and Cheese" and then add a final option: "Chicken Fingers."

14. Now put a check mark in the box next to **Make this a required question**.

15. Next, you can add another question by clicking the **Add Item** button at the top-left corner of the page (Figure 14-6). Choose **Checkboxes**.

Figure 14-6

16. You can also click on the **Duplicate** icon (Figure 14-7). This will add a question that is exactly like the previous question into your form.

Figure 14-7

17. Type your third question in the Question Title box: "Which of the following is your favorite ice cream flavor?"

18. Now, in the **Help Text** box, type "Please pick only one choice."

19. Next, click on the **Question Type** drop-down menu and select the **Choose from a list** option.

20. Click into the **Option 1** box and type "Chocolate." Then hit the **Enter** key on your keyboard to create an **Option 2** box (Figure 14-8).

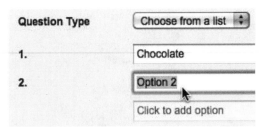

Figure 14-8

21. Type "Strawberry" in the **Option 2** box.

22. Add a third option to your form and type "Vanilla" in the **Option 3** box.

23. Put a check in the **Make this a required question** box, then click **Done**.

24. Using the **Add Item** button on the upper-left of your form, choose **Checkboxes** from the **Question Type** drop-down menu.

25. In the **Question Title** box, type "Which drink do you like most?"

26. In the **Help Text** box, enter "Choose only one."

Favorite Foods Survey *(cont.)*

Activity 14

27. Click into the **Option 1** box and type "Water." Click into the **Option 2** box and type "Juice." Add two more options, "Milk," and "Soda" (Figure 14-9).

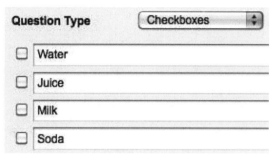

Figure 14-9

28. Make sure to check **Make this a required question**, then click **Done**.

29. Finally, insert one last question into your form. Make this a **Scale** question (Figure 14-10).

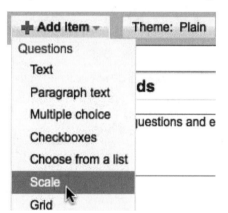

Figure 14-10

30. Enter the following in the **Question Title** box, "How spicy do you like your food?"

31. Now you must set the scale to answer this question. Set the scale from **1** to **10** using the drop-down menus (Figure 14-11).

Figure 14-11

32. Now type a description of the scale. Under the **Labels** option in the first box, type "Mild (not hot at all)."

Activity 14

33. In the second box, type "Very Spicy (I'm crying!)" (Figure 14-12).

Figure 14-12

34 Put a check mark in the **Make this a required question** box. Your form is now complete. Click the **Done** button.

35. Next, you are going to change the theme of your form. Changing a theme changes the appearance of your form. It changes the background and format. To change the theme, click the **Theme** button located at the upper-right of your form (Figure 14-13).

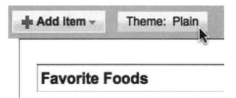

Figure 14-13

36. Clicking the **Theme** button brings up many different ways to display your form. Choose the **Letterhead** theme, and then click the **Apply** button at the top left of the page. Your theme is now set.

37. Next, you will make a list of email contacts to whom you will send your questionnaire. Click on the **Email this form** button at the upper-right of your form (Figure 14-14)

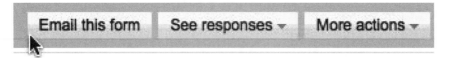

Figure 14-14

38. In the **Send this form to others** window, enter the email addresses provided by your teacher. Then click **Send**. Your form will now be emailed to your classmates. You can click on the **See responses** button to view the results. Your project is now complete!

A Famous American

Activity 15

Objectives

Each student will utilize the Google Docs presentation application to create a presentation about a famous American.

Benchmarks for Technology Standards

Students will know the characteristics, uses, and basic features of computer software programs, including:

- using the common features of desktop publishing and word-processing software
- knowing that documents can be created, designed, and formatted, and that data and graphics can be imported

Learning Objectives

At the end of this lesson, students will be able to:

1. create a new presentation document
2. know the various terms associated with presentations, including slides, theme, slide show, normal view, title, and subtitle
3. select a theme for a presentation
4. insert a title into a presentation
5. insert a subtitle into a presentation
6. insert a bulleted list into a presentation
7. insert an image into a presentation
8. insert a caption into a presentation
9. change the size of the font within a presentation
10. create a new slide within a presentation
11. view the presentation as a slide show
12. download the presentation in different formats

Before the Computer

This activity is written using astronaut Neil Armstrong as the famous American, but you may choose to have your students research other people prior to beginning this activity and substitute them when creating their presentations. An example set of presentation slides for this activity is shown in Figure 15-1.

Neil Armstrong

A Famous American
by Sally Student

Neil Armstrong's Early Life

- Neil Armstrong was born on August 5, 1930 in Ohio.
- He worked in a pharmacy to earn money for flying lessons when he was 14 years old.
- Neil received his pilot's license on his 16th birthday.
- He attended Purdue University and studied Aeronautical Engineering.
- Neil flew 78 combat missions during the Korean War.

Neil Armstrong, Test Pilot

Neil became a test pilot in 1955 and flew over 200 different types of aircraft, including the 4,000 mph X-15.

Neil Armstrong Joins NASA

Neil Armstrong became an astronaut for NASA in 1962. He commanded the *Gemini 8* mission, which was the first to dock together two vehicles in space.

On July 20, 1969, he became the first human to walk on the moon.

Figure 15-1

Procedure

1. Open a new presentation document in Google Docs.

2. At the top of the document in the **Untitled Presentation** box, type your last name and the title "Famous American" (Figure 15-2). Click **OK**.

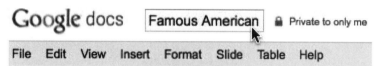

Figure 15-2

3. Next, you are going to set the theme for your presentation. A theme is a specific format for a presentation which is applied to all slides. Select the **Format** menu, **Presentation settings**, and choose **Change theme** (Figure 15-3).

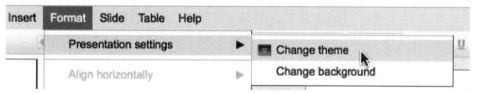

Figure 15-3

4. In the **Choose theme** window, select **Gradient White**.

5. Now that you have set up your theme, click into the **Click to add title** box and type "Neil Armstrong."

6. Next, click into the **Click to add subtitle** box and type "A Famous American."

7. Now hit the **Enter** key on your keyboard, type "by," and then type your first and last name (Figure 15-4).

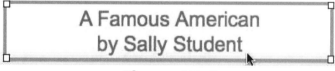

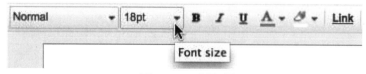

Figure 15-4

8. Next, click and drag over the word "by" and your name to highlight it. Then reduce its font size to **18** using the **Font size** button (Figure 15-5).

Figure 15-5

A Famous American (cont.)

Activity 15

9. Now go to the **Slide** menu and select **New slide** (Figure 15-6).

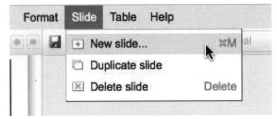

Figure 15-6

10. In the **Choose slide layout** window, select **Text** (Figure 15-7).

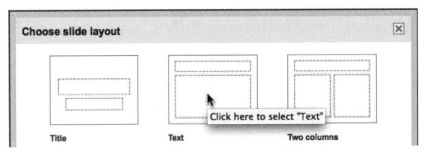

Figure 15-7

11. Your new slide should now have been inserted into your presentation. Click into the **Click to add title box** and type "Neil Armstrong's Early Life."

12. Next, click into the **Click to add content box** and type "Neil Armstrong was born on August 5, 1930 in Ohio."

13. Now you are going to make your text appear as a list. Keep your cursor at the end of the sentence, and click the **Bullet list** button (Figure 15-8).

Figure 15-8

14. Hit the **Enter** key on your keyboard. Your text should now appear in a bullet list.

15. On the next line, type "He worked in a pharmacy to earn money for flying lessons when he was 14 years old."

16. Add another line to your list and type "Neil received his pilot's license on his 16th birthday."

17. Hit **Enter** on your keyboard and add another fact: "He attended Purdue University and studied Aeronautical Engineering."

18. Type this final fact about Neil Armstrong's early life: "Neil flew 78 combat missions during the Korean War."

A Famous American *(cont.)*

Activity 15

19. Next, you will insert an image into the slide. There are two ways to insert images into a slide. First, you can select an image that is stored on your computer by choosing the **Insert** menu, and selecting **Image** (Figure 15-9).

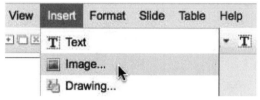

Figure 15-9

20. You can then use the **Insert Image** window to navigate to the image file on your computer.

21. Another way to insert an image is using Google's Image Search to locate an image. Then you can just click and drag it onto your slide. To do this, go to the **File** menu of your web browser and choose **New Window** (Figure 15-10).

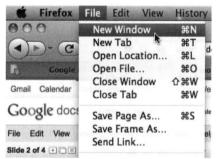

Figure 15-10

22. Next, navigate to Google at **http://www.google.com**. Click the **Images** search link at the top of the page, then type "Neil Armstrong" into the **Search Images** box and hit the **Search** button.

23. Your image search should have produced many images of Neil Armstrong. Click the bottom-corner of your web browser to minimize it so it takes up only half of your screen. Then click and drag an image of Neil Armstrong onto your slide (Figure 15-11).

Figure 15-11

24. Your image should now be inserted into your slide. Click and drag the image so it is positioned near the bottom center of the slide. Use the anchor points to reduce its size so it fits (Figure 15-12).

• Neil flew 78 combat missions during the Korean War.

Figure 15-12

25. Next, insert a new **Text** slide and add the following title, "Neil Armstrong, Test Pilot." Use the **Center** button to center the title (Figure 15-13).

Center

Figure 15-13

26. Click in the **Click to add content** box and type the following paragraph: "Neil Armstrong became a test pilot in 1955 and flew over 200 different types of aircraft, including the 4,000 mph X-15." Highlight the text and center it. Also use the **Font size** menu to increase the font size to **24 pt** (Figure 15-14).

Normal 24pt **B** *I* U A
Font size

Figure 15-14

27. Return to the Google Image Search window you used to find an image of Neil Armstrong, and now perform a new image search. Type "X-15 plane" in the search box.

28. When you find an image of an X-15, click and drag it onto your slide, centered below the text (Figure 15-15).

Neil Armstrong, Test Pilot

Neil became a test pilot in 1955 and flew over 200
different types of aircraft, including the 4,000 mph
X-15.

Figure 15-15

29. Next, insert a new **Text** slide and add the following title, "Neil Armstrong Joins NASA." Highlight and center the text.

30. Click down into the **Click to add content** box and type the following paragraph: "Neil Armstrong became an astronaut for NASA in 1962. He commanded the Gemini 8 mission, which was the first to dock together two space vehicles in space." Center this text. Highlight "Gemini 8" and click on the **Italic (I)** button to italicize it.

31. Return to your Google Image Search window and type the following search term: "Neil Armstrong."

32. Choose an image of Neil Armstrong in his space suit without his helmet, then drag it onto your slide. Center and resize it under the text.

33. Next, insert a new **Caption** slide (Figure 15-16) and add the following caption: "On July 20, 1969, he became the first human to walk on the moon!"

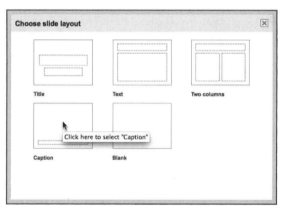

Figure 15-16

34. Finally, return to the Google Image Search window and drag an image of Neil Armstrong on the moon onto your slide. Center and re-size it above your caption.

35. To view your slide show, click the **Start presentation** button located at the top-right corner of your page (Figure 15-17).

Figure 15-17

36. Your project is complete! You can also download your presentation in different formats by selecting the **File** menu and choosing **Download As** (Figure 15-18).

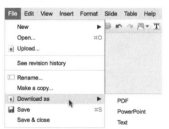

Figure 15-18

Simple Machines

Activity 16

Objectives

Each student will utilize the Google Docs presentation application to create a presentation about five simple machines.

Benchmarks for Technology Standards

Students will know the characteristics, uses, and basic features of computer software programs, including:

- using the common features of desktop publishing and word processing software
- knowing that documents can be created, designed, and formatted, and that data and graphics can be imported

Learning Objectives

At the end of this lesson, students will be able to:

1. create a new presentation document
2. know the various terms associated with presentations, including slides, theme, slide show, normal view, title, and subtitle
3. select a theme for a presentation
4. insert a title into a presentation
5. insert a subtitle into a presentation
6. insert a bulleted list into a presentation
7. insert a drawing into a presentation
8. change the size of the font within a presentation
9. create a new slide within a presentation
10. view the presentation as a slide show
11. download a presentation in different file formats

Before the Computer

It might be helpful for students to research the five simple machines prior to this activity so they are familiar with how they work. Also, if your class has used the Google Docs presentation application before, you may wish to have small groups of students work together and collaborate on one document. Refer to the introduction to this workbook to learn how students can work on one presentation simultaneously. An example set of presentation slides for this activity is shown in Figure 16-1.

Simple Machines (cont.)

Activity 16

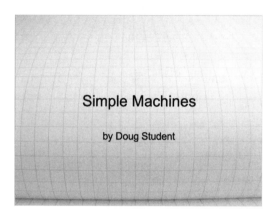

Simple Machines

by Doug Student

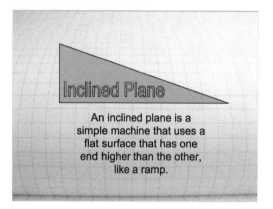

Inclined Plane

An inclined plane is a simple machine that uses a flat surface that has one end higher than the other, like a ramp.

Screw

A screw uses spiraled grooves within a cylinder, also known as threads, which work much like an inclined plane. When the screw is turned, the grooves move the cylinder forward.

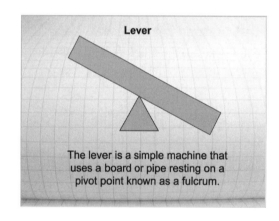

Lever

The lever is a simple machine that uses a board or pipe resting on a pivot point known as a fulcrum.

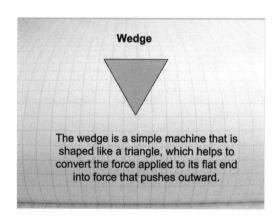

Wedge

The wedge is a simple machine that is shaped like a triangle, which helps to convert the force applied to its flat end into force that pushes outward.

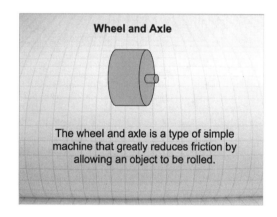

Wheel and Axle

The wheel and axle is a type of simple machine that greatly reduces friction by allowing an object to be rolled.

Figure 16-1

Simple Machines (cont.)

Activity 16

Procedure

1. Open a new presentation document in Google Docs.

2. At the top of the document in the **Untitled Presentation** box, type your last name and the title "Simple Machines." Click **OK**.

3. Next, you are going to set the theme for your presentation. A theme is a specific format for a presentation, which is applied to all slides within your presentation. Select the **Format** menu, **Presentation Settings**, and choose **Change Theme** (Figure 16-2).

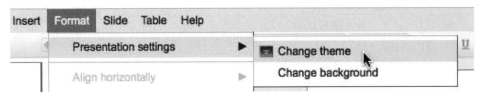

Figure 16-2

4. In the **Choose theme** window, select **Graph Paper**.

5. Now that you have set up your theme, click into the **Click to add title** box and type "Simple Machines."

6. Next, click into the **Click to add subtitle** box, type the word "by," and then enter your first and last name or the name of your group members (Figure 16-3).

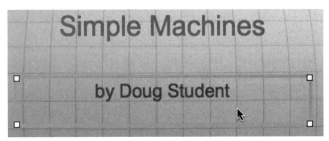

Figure 16-3

7. Now go to the **Slide** menu and select **New slide** (Figure 16-4).

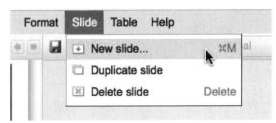

Figure 16-4

8. In the **Choose slide** layout window, select **Blank**.

9. Your new slide should now be inserted into your presentation.

10. Next, choose the **Insert** menu and select **Drawing**. This will bring up the **Insert Drawing** window, which allows you to use the same types of drawing tools as in the Google Docs drawing application.

11. Click on the **Shape** button, select **Shapes**, and choose the **Right Triangle** (Figure 16-5).

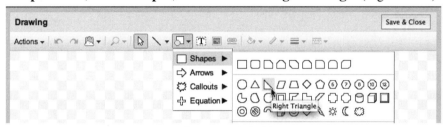

Figure 16-5

12. Use the triangle tool to draw a large inclined plane (Figure 16-6).

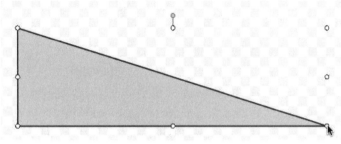

Figure 16-6

13. Change the fill color of the shape to gray by using the **Fill color** button (Figure 16-7).

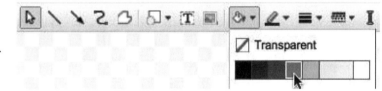

Figure 16-7

14. Also change the line color of your shape to black by using the **Line color** button (Figure 16-8).

Figure 16-8

15. Next, you will create a label for your shape using the **Word Art** tool. Click on the **Actions** button and select **Word Art** (Figure 16-9).

Figure 16-9

16. Type the following into the **Word Art** text box: "Inclined Plane." Hit the **Enter** key on your keyboard.

17. Use the anchor points on the **Word Art** text box to reduce the size of the text so that it fits within the inclined plane (Figure 16-10).

Figure 16-10

18. Now you will insert your drawing onto your slide. To do this, click the **Save & Close** button located at the top-right of the drawing window. The drawing should now appear within your slide.

19. Next, you will insert a text box below the drawing. To do this, select the **Insert** menu and choose **Text**.

20. In the text box, type the following information about an inclined plane: "An inclined plane is a simple machine that uses a flat surface that has one end higher than the other, like a ramp."

21. Highlight the text within your textbox, center it using the **Center** align button and increase its font size to **26** using the **Font size** button (Figure 16-11).

Figure 16-11

22. Now click and drag the textbox so it is centered below your drawing of the inclined plane.

23. Next, insert a new **Blank** slide into your presentation.

24. Now you will insert an image into the slide. There are two ways to insert images into a slide. First, you can select an image that is stored on your computer by choosing the **Insert** menu, and selecting **Image** (Figure 16-12).

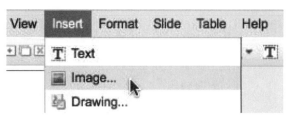

Figure 16-12

Simple Machines (cont.)

Activity 16

25. You can then use the **Insert Image** window to navigate to the image file on your computer.

26. You can also use Google's Image Search to locate an image. Then you can just click and drag it into your slide. To do this, go to the **File** menu of your web browser and choose **New Window** (Figure 16-13).

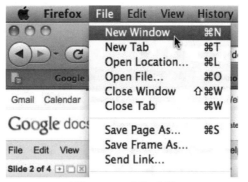

Figure 16-13

27. Next, navigate to the following web address: **http://www.google.com**. Click the **Images** link at the top of the page, then type "simple machine screw" into the **Search Images** box and hit the **Search** button.

28. Your image search should have produced many images of screws. Click the bottom-corner of your web browser to minimize it so it takes up only half of your screen. Then click and drag an image of a screw onto your slide (Figure 16-14).

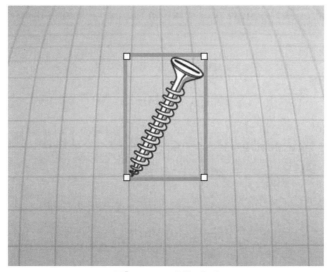

Figure 16-14

29. Your image should now be inserted into your slide. Click and drag the image so it is positioned near the top-center of the slide. Use the anchor points to increase its size so it fits in the middle of the slide.

30. Insert a textbox below the image of the screw. In the textbox type the following information about a screw, "A screw uses spiraled grooves within a cylinder, also known as threads, which work much like an inclined plane. When the screw is turned, the grooves move the cylinder forward."

31. Center the text and increase its font size to **26** (Figure 16-15).

Figure 16-15

32. Now that you know how to insert drawings into a slide, create three new slides with drawings and information about a lever, wedge, and the wheel and axle.

33. When you are finished with your presentation, you can view it as a slide show.

34. To view your slide show, click the **Start presentation** button located at the top right corner of your page (Figure 16-16).

Figure 16-16

35. Your project is complete! You can also download your presentation in different formats by selecting the **File** menu and choosing **Download as** (Figure 16-17).

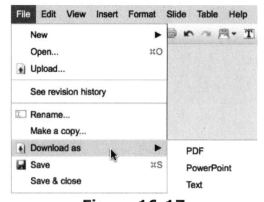

Figure 16-17